ACADEMIC LEGAL WRITING:

LAW REVIEW ARTICLES, STUDENT NOTES, AND SEMINAR PAPERS

by

EUGENE VOLOKH
Professor of Law
UCLA School of Law

with foreword by

JUDGE ALEX KOZINSKI
U.S. Court of Appeals for the Ninth Circuit

FOUNDATION PRESS
NEW YORK, NEW YORK
2003

THOMSON
WEST

COPYRIGHT © 2003 By FOUNDATION PRESS
　　　　　　　　395 Hudson Street
　　　　　　　　New York, NY 10014
　　　　　　　　Phone Toll Free 1–877–888–1330
　　　　　　　　Fax (212) 367–6799
　　　　　　　　fdpress.com

ISBN 1–58778–477–7

To my beloved wife,

Leslie Pereira

*

ABOUT THE AUTHOR

Eugene Volokh is a Professor of Law at UCLA, where he teaches First Amendment law, copyright law, and firearms regulation policy. Before going into teaching, he clerked for Ninth Circuit Judge Alex Kozinski and for Justice Sandra Day O'Connor.

Since 1995, he has published over 30 law review articles and over 40 op-eds in publications such as the *Harvard Law Review, Yale Law Journal, Stanford Law Review, Wall Street Journal, New York Times, Washington Post, New Republic,* and many others. He is also the author of *The First Amendment,* a textbook from Foundation Press, and he operates a daily Web log called *The Volokh Conspiracy (http://volokh.com).* Before going into law, he published over a dozen technical articles in computer magazines.

His student article, *Freedom of Speech and Workplace Harassment* (UCLA L. Rev. 1992), has been cited in over 140 academic works and 10 court cases. A 2002 survey by University of Texas law professor Brian Leiter listed him as the third most cited professor among those who entered law teaching after 1992 (with 810 citations in law reviews).

*

TABLE OF CONTENTS

II. SEMINAR TERM PAPERS

III. RESEARCH

IV. WRITING

VIII. ACADEMIC ETHICS

CONCLUSION

APPENDIX I: CLUMSY WORDS AND PHRASES

APPENDIX II: ANSWERS TO EXERCISES

TABLE OF CONTENTS

APPENDIX III: SAMPLE COVER LETTERS

*

ACADEMIC LEGAL WRITING:

LAW REVIEW ARTICLES, STUDENT NOTES, AND SEMINAR PAPERS

FOREWORD, BY JUDGE ALEX KOZINSKI

A few years ago I interviewed a candidate for a clerkship. He had record-breaking grades from a name-brand law school and his recommenders sprinkled their letters with phrases like "Kozinski clone" and "better even than you." This kid was hot.

His interview went well, and I had pretty much made up my mind to hire him on the spot, when I popped a fateful question: "So, have you decided on the topic for your law review note?"

"It's done," the candidate replied. And, with a flourish, he pulled an inch-thick document from his briefcase and plopped it on my desk. Impressed, I picked it up and read the title page: "The Alienability and Devisability of Possibilities of Reverter and Rights of Entry."

After making sure this wasn't a joke, I started wondering why someone would write a piece on such an arcane topic. Maybe this kid wasn't so smart after all. I decided I had better read the piece before making a hiring decision.

After the applicant left, his article sat on the corner of my desk like a brick. Every so often, I'd pick it up, leaf through it and try to read it, but with no success. It was well-written enough; the sentences were easy to understand and followed one another in seemingly logical fashion. But the effort was pointless because the subject matter was of absolutely no interest to me. Instead, my mind wandered to doubts about the author. How did he come to write on such a desiccated topic? Under that veneer of brilliance, was there a kook trying to get out? Could I really trust his judgment as to the countless sensitive issues he would have to confront during his clerkship? Would he constantly aim for the capillary and miss the jugular?

It is difficult to overstate the importance of a written paper for a young lawyer's career, especially if the piece is published. Grades, of necessity, are somewhat grainy and subjective; is an A− that much better than a B+? Letters of recommendation can be more useful, but they still rely on someone else's judgment, and they often have a stale booster quality about them. Words like "fabulous" and "extraordinary" lose their force by dint of repetition—though "Kozinski clone" is still pretty rare.

A paper is very different. It is the applicant's raw work product, unfiltered through a third-party evaluator. By reading it, you can personally evaluate the student's writing, research, logic and judgment. Are

1

the sentences sleek and lithe or ponderous and convoluted? Does he lay out his argument in a logical fashion, and does he anticipate and refute objections? Is the topic broad enough to be useful, yet narrow enough to be adequately covered? Is it persuasive? Is it fun to read? Writing a paper engages so much of the lawyer's art that no other predictor of likely success on the job comes close. A well-written, well-researched, thoughtful paper can clinch that law firm job or clerkship. It is indispensable if you aim to teach.

Published student papers can also be quite useful and influential in the development of the law. A few law review notes and comments become classics cited widely by lawyers, courts and academics. Many more provide a useful service, such as a solid body of research or an important insight into a developing area. Most, however, are read by no one beyond the student's immediate family and cause hardly an eddy among the currents of the law.

Why do so many published student papers fail in their essential purpose? (The same question might well be asked about non-student academic writing.) The simple answer is that most students have no clue what to write about, or how to go about writing it. Finding a useful and interesting topic; determining the scope of the paper; developing a thesis and testing its viability; avoiding sudden death through preemption; and getting it placed in the best possible journal—these are among the tasks that most students aren't trained to perform. My applicant, smart though he was, went off track because no one showed him where the track was or how to stay on it. Many students make the same mistake every year.

This book fills a void in the legal literature: It teaches students how to go about finding a topic and developing it into a useful, interesting, publishable piece. It gives detailed and very helpful instructions for every aspect of the writing, research and publication process. And it comes from the keyboard of someone who has authored articles on a dizzying variety of legal topics and is widely regarded as one of the brightest lights in legal academia.

But I digress.

I pondered the fate of my applicant for some weeks and never did get myself to read more than a few lines of his dreary paper. Finally I called and offered him a clerkship with a strong hint—not quite a condition—that he drop the paper in the nearest trash can and start from scratch. I explained to him what was wrong with it, and what a successful paper should look like. "You can do whatever you want," I told him, "but if you should have the misfortune of getting this dog

2

published, it will only drag you down when you apply for a Supreme Court clerkship or a position as a law professor."

The applicant gratefully accepted the advice. He chucked the "Possibilities of Reverter" paper and went about developing a new topic. Some months later, he produced a dynamite piece that became one of the seminal published articles in a developing area of the law. Eventually, he did clerk for the Supreme Court and has since become a widely respected and often quoted legal academic. His name is Eugene Volokh.

*

INTRODUCTION

A good student article can get you a high grade, a good law review editorial board position, and a publication credit. These credentials can in turn help get you jobs, clerkships, and—if you're so inclined—teaching positions. The experience will hone your writing, which is probably a lawyer's most important skill. Likewise, a good article written while you're clerking or in your early years as a practicing lawyer can impress employers (academic and otherwise) and clients.

And your article may influence judges, lawyers, and legislators. Law is one of the few disciplines where second-year graduate students write (not just cowrite) scholarly articles; and these articles are often taken seriously by others in the profession. Lawyers read them, scholars discuss them, and courts—including the U.S. Supreme Court—cite them. Occasionally, student articles and articles by young practicing lawyers have a huge impact; WESTLAW searches show that:

- Anthony Amsterdam's student article, *The Void-for-Vagueness Doctrine in the Supreme Court* (U. Pa. L. Rev. 1960), has been cited by over 250 scholarly works (and doubtless many more in the pre-WESTLAW era) and over 250 cases.

- Lewis Sargentich's student article, *The First Amendment Overbreadth Doctrine* (Harv. L. Rev. 1970), has been cited by nearly 200 scholarly works and over 150 cases.

- Naomi Sheiner's student article, *DES and a Proposed Theory of Enterprise Liability* (Fordham L. Rev. 1978), helped pioneer the concept of enterprise liability, has been cited by nearly 100 scholarly works and over 35 cases, and was heavily used by *Sindell v. Abbott Laboratories*, the leading case on the subject.

- Daniel Meltzer's student article, *Standing to Assert Constitutional Jus Tertii* (Harv. L. Rev. 1974), has been cited by nearly 60 scholarly works and nearly 60 cases.

- Robert F. Nagel's student article, *Legislative Purpose, Rationality, and Equal Protection* (Yale L.J. 1972), has been cited by over 75 scholarly works and 25 cases.

- Rachel Godsil's student article, *Remedying Environmental Racism* (Mich. L. Rev. 1991), has been cited by over 130 academic works.

Writing an article, whether as a law review note, as an independent study project, or as a side project in your first years in practice, is also one of the hardest things you will do. Your pre-law-school writing experience and your first-year writing class will help prepare you for it, but only partly. It's not easy to create an original scholarly work that contributes to our understanding of the law.

Seminar papers tend to be less ambitious and less time-consuming, partly because they don't have to be publishable. But they too help improve your writing—and if you invest enough effort into writing them, you can then easily make them publishable, even if publication isn't a seminar requirement.

In this book, I try to give some advice, based on my own writing experience and on discussions with others, for you to combine with other advice you get. These ideas have worked for me, and I hope they work for you.

Different parts of this book relate to different stages of your project. I suggest that you:

1. Start by reading Part I, about law review articles generally, and Part VIII, on academic ethics.

2. Read the short Part II as well, if you're writing a seminar term paper.

3. Once you identify a potential topic, read Part III, on research, and Parts V.A–V.F and V.J–V.K, on using evidence correctly. If you also plan to use survey evidence, read Part V.G, and if you plan to use other social science evidence, read Parts V.H–V.I.

4. When you're ready to start writing—which I hope you will be, soon—read Part IV.

5. As you get close to the end of your first draft, consider rereading Part I again, to see how you can improve your article in light of what you've learned while you were writing it.

6. If you're a law journal staffer or editor, read Parts V and VI to help you understand how to better cite-check others' articles, as well as how to better write your own.

7. When you're ready to publish the article, or publish the seminar paper that you've turned into a publishable article, read Part VII.

For more advice, read ELIZABETH FAJANS & MARY R. FALK, SCHOLARLY WRITING FOR LAW STUDENTS: SEMINAR PAPERS, LAW REVIEW NOTES, AND LAW REVIEW COMPETITION PAPERS (2000); Pamela Samuelson, *Good Legal Writing: Of Orwell and Window Panes*, 46 U. PITT. L. REV. 149 (1984); and Richard Delgado, *How to Write a Law Review Article*, 20 U.S.F. L. REV. 445 (1986).

ACKNOWLEDGMENTS

Many thanks to Bruce Adelstein, Alison Anderson, Stuart Benjamin, Paul Bergman, David Binder, Dan Bussel, Stephen Calkins, Cassandra Franklin, Eric Freedman, Dana Gardner, Bryan Garner, Ken Graham, Sharon Gold, Brian Kalt, Pam Karlan, Orin Kerr, Ken Klee, Kris Knaplund, Terri LeClercq, Sandy Levinson, Nancy Levit, Jim Lindgren, Dan Lowenstein, Elaine Mandel, Steve Munzer, Steve Postrel, Greg Schwinghammer, David Sklansky, Bill Somerfeld, Lauren Teukolsky, Rebecca Tushnet, Vladimir Volokh, Alysa Wakin, Bruce Wessel, Virginia Wise, Steve Yeazell, and Amy Zegart for their advice; to the UCLA Law Library staff—especially Laura Cadra, Xia Chen, Maureen Dunnigan, Kevin Gerson, Jennifer Lentz, Cynthia Lewis, and John Wilson—for all their help; and to Leib Lerner for his thoughtful and thorough editing and cite-checking. And, of course, my deepest thanks to Judge Alex Kozinski, who taught me most of what I know about legal writing.

*

I. Law Review Articles and Student Notes: The Basics

A. *The Initial Step: Choosing a Claim*

Good legal scholarship should make (1) a claim that is (2) novel, (3) nonobvious, (4) useful, (5) sound, and (6) seen by the reader to be novel, nonobvious, useful, and sound.*

This is true whether the author is a student, a young lawyer, a seasoned expert, or an academic. I will sometimes allude below to student authors (since I expect that most readers of this book will be students), for instance by discussing grades or faculty advisors. But nearly all of this book should apply equally to other aspiring academic writers.

1. The Claim

a. Your basic thesis

Most good works of original scholarship have a basic thesis—a claim they are making about the world. This could be a *descriptive* claim about the world as it is or as it was (such as a historical assertion, a claim about a law's effects, a statement about how courts are interpreting a law, or the like). It could be a *prescriptive* claim about what should be done (how a law or a constitutional provision should be interpreted, what new statute should be enacted, how a statute or a common-law rule should be changed, or the like). It could also be a combination of both a descriptive claim and a prescriptive one. In any case, you should be able to condense that claim into one sentence, for instance:

- "Law X is unconstitutional because . . . ."
- "The legislature ought to enact the following statute: . . . ."
- "Properly interpreted, this statute means . . . ."
- "This law is likely to have the following side effects . . . ."
- "This law is likely to have the following side effects . . ., and therefore should be rejected or modified to say . . . ."

---

* I am indebted for much of this formulation to Stephen L. Carter, *Academic Tenure and "White Male" Standards: Some Lessons from the Patent Law*, 100 YALE L.J. 2065, 2083 (1991).

9

- "Courts have interpreted the statute in the following ways ...,
  and therefore the statute should be amended as follows ...."

- "My empirical research shows that this law has unexpectedly led
  to ..., and it should therefore be changed this way ...."

- "My empirical research shows that this law has had the following
  good effects ..., and should therefore be kept, or extended to
  other jurisdictions."

- "Viewing this law from a [feminist/Catholic/economic] perspective
  leads us to conclude that the law is flawed, and should be changed
  this way ...."

Capturing your point in a single sentence helps you focus your
discussion, and helps you communicate your core point to the readers.
Moreover, many readers will remember only one sentence about your
article (especially if they only read the Introduction, as many readers
do). You need to understand what you want that sentence to be, so you
can frame your article in a way that will help readers absorb your main
point.

b. The descriptive and the prescriptive parts of the thesis

The most interesting claims are often ones that combine the descriptive and the prescriptive, telling readers something they didn't know
about the world—whether it's about what courts have done, how a legal
rule changes people's behavior, or why a rule has developed in a
particular way—but also suggesting what should be done. The descriptive is valuable because many people are more persuadable by novel facts
than by novel moral or legal arguments. The prescriptive is valuable
because it answers the inevitable "so what?" question that many practically minded readers will ask whenever they hear a factual description,
even a very interesting one.

You can certainly write an article that's purely prescriptive or
purely descriptive (though see Part I.A.7.d, p. 29 for a discussion of one
sort of descriptive piece that you might want to avoid). Combining the
prescriptive and the descriptive, however, tends to yield a more interesting and impressive article. So as you're developing your claim, try to look
both for novel, nonobvious, useful, and sound descriptive assertions and
for novel, nonobvious, useful, and sound prescriptions.

c. Identifying a problem

To get to a claim, you must first identify a problem, whether a doctrinal, empirical, or historical one, in a general area that interests you; the claim will then be your proposed solution to that problem. Some tips:

1. Think back on *cases you've read for class* that led you to think "this leaves an important question unresolved" or "the reasoning here is unpersuasive."

2. Try to recall *class discussions* that intrigued you but didn't yield a well-settled answer.

3. Read the *questions that many casebooks include* after each case; these questions often identify interesting unsolved problems. Look not just at the casebook that you used yourself, but also at other leading casebooks in the field.

4. Read *recent Supreme Court cases* in fields that interest you, and see whether they leave open major issues or create new ambiguities or uncertainties.

5. Ask *faculty members* which areas of the law they think have been unduly neglected by scholars; some (though not all) of the professors you ask may even suggest specific problems.

6. Ask *practicing lawyers* which important unsettled questions they find themselves facing.

7. Check the *Westlaw Bulletin* (WLB), *Westlaw State Bulletin* (WSB–CA, WSB–NY, and such), and *Westlaw Topical Highlights* (WTH–CJ, WTH–IP, and such) databases. These databases summarize, in one paragraph each, noteworthy recent cases; many such cases contain legal developments that might prove worth analyzing.

8. Check *http://www.lawtopic.org*, a law review topics clearing house that the UCLA Law Library and I have put together.

9. Read Heather Meeker's *Stalking the Golden Topic: A Guide to Locating and Selecting Topics for Legal Research Papers*, 1996 UTAH L. REV. 917.

Look for a problem that's big enough to be important and interesting but small enough to be manageable.

d. Checking with your law school's faculty

Once you've tentatively chosen a problem, run it by your faculty adviser. Your adviser will probably know better than you do whether there's already too much written on the subject, or whether there's less substance to the problem than you might think.

Also talk to other faculty members at your school who teach in the field, even if you don't know them. Most are happy to spend a few minutes helping a student.

Even if you're no longer a student, you should still be able to draw on your law school's faculty: Professors feel some obligation to help alumni, especially those who they think will eventually try to go into teaching. If you feel uncomfortable approaching a faculty member whom you don't know, ask another professor whom you do know to introduce you (in person or electronically).

e. Keeping an open mind

Do your research with an open mind. Be willing to make whatever claims your reading and thinking lead you to.

Also be willing to change or refine the problem itself. Remember that your goal is to find whatever problem will yield the best article. Don't feel locked into a particular problem or solution just because it's the first one you thought of.

f. Identifying a tentative solution

Decide what seems to be the best solution to the problem. For the descriptive part of your claim, the best solution is just the most plausible explanation of the facts (about history, about the way the law has been applied, about the way people behave) that you've uncovered.

For the prescriptive part, the best solution could be a new statute, a new constitutional rule, a new common law rule, a new interpretation of a statute, a new enforcement practice, a novel application of a general principle to a certain kind of case, or the like. This will be your *claim*: "State legislatures should enact the following statute ...." "Courts should interpret this constitutional provision this way ...." "This law should be seen as unconstitutional in these cases ..., but constitutional in those ...."

Test your solution against several factual scenarios you've found in the cases, and against several other hypotheticals you can think up. Does the solution yield the results that you think are right? Does it seem determinate enough to be consistently applied by judges, juries, or executive officials? If the answer to either question is "no," change your solution to make it more correct and more clear. (I discuss this "test suite" process further at p. 19.)

The solution doesn't have to be perfect: It's fine to propose a rule even when you have misgivings about the results it will produce in a few unusual cases. But candidly testing your solution against the factual scenarios will tell you whether even you yourself find the solution plausible. If you don't, your readers won't, either.

2. Novelty

a. Adding to the body of professional knowledge

To be valuable, your article must be novel: It must say something that hasn't been said before by others. It's not enough for your ideas to be original to you, in the sense that you came up with them on your own—the article must add something to the state of expert knowledge about the field. It helps if your claim itself is novel, but at least your claim coupled with your basic rationale must be novel.

For instance, say you want to criticize obscenity law. Many people have already argued that obscenity law is unconstitutional because it interferes with self-expression, or because it's too vague. You shouldn't write yet another article that makes the same point.

But a new test for what should constitute unprotected obscenity might be a novel proposal (and might even be useful, if you argue that state supreme courts should adopt it even if the U.S. Supreme Court doesn't, see Part I.A.4.b, p. 17). So would a proposal that obscenity law should be entirely unconstitutional, if you've come up with a novel *justification* for your claim: For instance, the claim that "obscenity laws are unsound because, as a study I've done shows, such laws are usually enforced primarily against gay pornography" may well be novel. (This claim and the others I mention below are just examples. I don't vouch for their correctness, or recommend that you write about them.)

What if you've chosen your topic and your basic rationale, and, four weeks into your research, you find that someone else has said the same thing? No need to despair yet.

b. Making novelty through nuance

Often you can make your claim novel by making it more nuanced. For instance, don't just say, "bans on nonmisleading commercial advertising should be unconstitutional," but say (perhaps) "bans on nonmisleading commercial advertising should be unconstitutional unless minors form a majority of the intended audience for the advertising." The more complex your claim, the more likely it is that no one has made it before. Of course, you should make sure that the claim is still (a) useful and (b) correct.

Some tips for making your claim more nuanced:

1. Think about what special factors—for instance, government interests or individual rights—are present in some situations covered by your claim but not in others. Could you modify your claim to consider these factors?

2. Think about your arguments in support of your claim. Do they work well in some cases but badly in others? Perhaps you should limit your claim accordingly.

3. For most legal questions, both the simple "yes" answer and the simple "no" tend to attract a lot of writing. See if you can come up with a plausible answer that's somewhere in between—"yes" in some cases, "no" in others.

3. Nonobviousness

Say Congress is considering a proposed federal cause of action for libel on the Internet. You want to argue that such a law wouldn't violate the First Amendment.

Your claim would be novel, but pretty obvious. Most people you discuss it with will say, "you're right, but I could have told you that myself." Libel law, if properly limited, has repeatedly been held to be constitutional, and many people have already argued that libel law should be the same in cyberspace as outside it. Unless you can explain how federal cyber-libel law differs from state libel law applied to cyberspace, your point will seem banal.

Claims such as that one, which just apply settled law or well-established arguments to slightly new fact patterns, tend to look obvious. Keep in mind that your article will generally be read by smart and often slightly arrogant readers (your professor, the law review editors, other people working in the field) who will be tempted to say "well, I could have thought of that if I'd only taken fifteen minutes"—even when that's not quite true.

You can avoid obviousness by adding some twist that most observers would not have thought of. For example, might a federal cyber-libel law be not just constitutional, but also more efficient, because it sets a uniform nationwide standard? Could it be more efficient in some situations but not others? Could it interact unexpectedly with some other federal laws? Making your claim more nuanced can make it less obvious as well as more novel.

If you can, describe your claim to a faculty member who works in the field (besides your adviser), an honest classmate who's willing to criticize your ideas, and a lawyer who works in the field. If they think it's obvious, either refine your claim, or, if you're confident that the claim is in fact not obvious, refine your presentation to better show the claim's unexpected aspects.

4. Utility

You'll be investing a lot of time in your article. You'll also want readers to invest time in reading it. It helps if the article is useful—if at least some readers can come away from it with something that they'll find professionally valuable. And the more readers can benefit from it, the better.

a. Focus on issues left open

Say you think the U.S. Supreme Court's *Doe v. Roe* decision is wrong. You can write a brilliant piece about how the Court erred, and such an article might be useful to some academics. But *Doe* is the law, and unless the Court revisits the issue, few people will practically benefit from your insight.

You should ask yourself: How can I make my article more useful not just to radically minded scholars, but also to lawyers, judges, and scholars who aren't interested in challenging the existing Supreme Court caselaw here? One possibility is to identify questions that *Doe* left unresolved—or questions that it created—and explain how they should be resolved in light of *Doe*'s reasoning, along with the reasoning of several other Supreme Court cases in the field. Such an article would be useful to any lawyer, scholar, or judge who's considering a matter that involves one of these questions.

b. Apply your argument to other jurisdictions

Say *Doe* holds that a certain kind of police conduct doesn't violate the Fourth Amendment. This makes *Doe* binding precedent as to the Fourth Amendment, but only persuasive authority as to state constitutions, because courts can interpret state constitutions as providing more protection than the federal one.

The claim "state courts interpreting their own state constitutional protections should reach a different result" is therefore more useful than just "the Court got it wrong." Judges are more likely to accept the revised claim, lawyers are more likely to argue it, and academics are more likely to build on it. Your article will still be valuable to scholars who are willing to challenge the Court's case law, but it will also be valuable to many others.

c. Incorporate prescriptive implications of your descriptive findings

You can make a valuable contribution to knowledge just by uncovering some important facts: historical facts, facts about how a law is being applied, facts about how people behave, and so on. But your contribution would be still more valuable, and more impressive, if your claim also contained a prescription—an assertion about the way the law ought to be—based on these findings.

Practical-minded people who read a purely descriptive piece will often ask "So what?" If you answer this question for them, you'll increase the chances that they'll see your work as useful. Don't do this if it's too much of a stretch: If there are no clear modern implications of your findings about 14th century English property law, you're better off sticking just with your persuasive historical claims rather than adding an unpersuasive prescriptive claim. But if you see some prescriptive implications, work them in.

d. Consider making a more politically feasible proposal

Say your claim is quite radical, and you're sure that few people will accept it, no matter how effectively you argue. For instance, imagine you want to urge courts to apply strict scrutiny to restrictions on economic liberty—a step beyond *Lochner v. New York*. You may have a great argument for that, but courts probably won't be willing to adopt your theory.

Think about switching to a more modest claim. You might argue, for instance, that courts should apply strict scrutiny to restrictions on entering certain professions or businesses. This would be a less radical change, and you can also support it by using particular arguments that wouldn't work as well for the broader claim.

Maybe courts will still be unlikely to go that far. Can you argue for a lower (but still significant) level of scrutiny? Can you find precedents, perhaps under state constitutions, that support your theory, thus showing your critics that your theory is more workable than they might at first think?

Or perhaps you could limit your proposal to strict scrutiny for laws that interfere with the obligation of contracts, rather than for all economic restrictions. Here you have more support from the constitutional text, a narrower (and thus less radical-seeming) claim, and perhaps even some more support from state cases: It turns out that state courts have interpreted the contracts clauses of many state constitutions more strictly than the federal clause.

If you really want to make the radical claim, go ahead—you might start a valuable academic debate, and perhaps might even eventually prevail. But, on balance, claims that call for modest changes to current doctrine tend to be more useful than radical claims, especially in articles by students or by junior practitioners. By making a more moderate claim, you can remain true to your basic moral judgment while producing something that's much more likely to influence people. Many legal campaigns are most effectively fought through small, incremental steps.

e. Make sure the argument doesn't unnecessarily alienate your audience

You should try to make your argument as appealing as possible to as many readers as possible. You can't please everyone, but you should avoid using rhetoric, examples, or jargon that unnecessarily alienates readers who might otherwise be persuadable.

For instance, say that you're writing an article on free speech, and in passing give anti-abortion speech as an example. If you call this "anti-choice" speech, your readers will likely assume that you bitterly oppose the anti-abortion position. Some pro-life readers might therefore become less receptive to your other, more important, arguments; and even some pro-choice readers may bristle at the term "anti-choice" because they see it as an attempt to make a political point through labeling rather than through argument. If you're pro-choice, imagine your reaction to an article that in passing calls your position "anti-life"—would this make you more or less open to the article's other messages?

Avoid this by using language that's as neutral as possible. Right now, for instance, "pro-choice" and "pro-life" seem to cause the fewest visceral reactions; most terms have some political message embedded in them, but these seem to have the least, perhaps because repeated use has largely drained them of their emotional content. But in any case, find something that is acceptable both to you and to most of your readers.

The same goes for terms like "gun lobby," "gun-grabber," "abortionist," "fanatic," and the like. You may feel these terms are accurate, but that's not enough. Many readers will condemn these terms as attempts to resolve the issue through emotion rather than logic, and will therefore become less open to your substantive arguments. Likewise, if you're analogizing some views or actions to those of Nazis or Stalinists, you're asking for trouble unless the analogy is very close.

Try also to avoid using jargon that will confuse those who are unfamiliar with it, or that will unnecessarily label your work (fairly or unfairly) as belonging to some controversial school of analysis. If you have to use the jargon because you need it to clearly explain your theory, that's fine. But if you're writing an article on a topic that's not really focused on a specialized method such as law and economics, literary criticism, or feminist legal theory, then stay away from the terms characteristic of those disciplines. Replacing them with plain English will probably make your article clearer and more accessible, and will avoid bringing in the ideological connotations that some people see these terms as having.

Likewise, try to include some arguments or examples that broaden your article's political appeal. If you are making a seemingly conservative proposal, but you can persuasively argue that the proposal will help poor people, say so. If you are making a seemingly liberal proposal, but you can persuasively argue that the proposal fits with tradition or with the original meaning of the Constitution, say that.

You should of course be willing to make unpopular arguments, if you need them to support your claim; that's part of the scholar's job. And if you really want to engage in a particular side battle, you might choose to bring it up even if you don't strictly have to. But in general, don't weaken your core claim by picking unnecessary fights.

5. Soundness

a. Test suites

When you're making a prescriptive proposal (whether it's a new statute, an interpretation of a statute, a constitutional rule, a common-law rule, a regulation, or an enforcement guideline), it's often easy to get tunnel vision: You focus on the one situation that prompted you to write the piece—usually a situation about which you feel deeply—and ignore other scenarios to which your proposal might apply. And this can lead you to make proposals that, on closer examination, prove to be unsound.

For instance, say you're outraged by the government's funding childbirths but not abortions. You might therefore propose a new rule that "if the government funds the nonexercise of a constitutional right, then the government must also fund the exercise of the right"; or you might simply propose that "if the government funds childbirth, it must fund abortions," and give the more general claim as a justification. But you might not think about the consequences of this general claim—when the government funds public school education, it would also have to fund private school education (since that's also a constitutional right), and when it funds anti-drug speech, it might also have to fund pro-drug speech.

Your argument, at least at its initial level of generality, is thus probably wrong or at least incomplete. But focusing on your one core case keeps you from seeing the error.

One way to fight these errors is a device borrowed from computer programming: the *test suite*. A test suite is a set of cases that programmers enter into their programs to see whether the results look right. A test suite for a calculator program might contain the following test cases, among many others:

1. Check that $2+2$ yields 4.

2. Check that $3-1$ yields 2.

3. Check that $1-3$ yields -2 (because the program might work differently with positive numbers than with negative ones).

4. Check that $1 / 0$ yields an error message.

If all the test cases yield the correct result, then the programmer can have some confidence that the program works. If one test yields the wrong result, then the programmer sees the need to fix the program—not throw it out, but improve it. Such test suites are a fundamental part of sound software design. Before going into law, for instance, I wrote a computer program that had 50,000 lines of test suites for its 140,000 lines of code.

You can use a similar approach for testing legal proposals. *Before* you commit yourself to a particular proposal, you should design a test suite containing various cases to which your proposal might apply.*

Assume, for instance, that you are upset by peyote bans that interfere with some American Indian religions. The government has no business, you want to argue, imposing such paternalistic laws on religious observers. You should design a set of test cases involving requests for religious exemptions from many different kinds of paternalistic laws, for instance:

1. requests for religious exemptions from assisted suicide bans, sought by a doctor who wants to help a dying patient die, or by the patient who wants a doctor's help;

2. requests for religious exemptions from assisted suicide bans, sought by a physically healthy cult member who wants help committing suicide;

3. requests for religious exemptions from bans on the drinking of strychnine (an example of extremely dangerous behavior);

4. requests for religious exemptions from bans on the handling of poisonous snakes (an example of less dangerous behavior);

5. requests for religious exemptions from bans on riding motorcycles without a helmet (an example of less dangerous behavior, but one that—unlike in examples 3 and 4—many nonreligious people want to engage in).[1†]

Then, once you design a proposed rule, you should test it by applying it to all these cases and seeing what results the proposal reaches.

b. What you might find by testing your proposals

What information can this testing provide?

1. *Error:* You might find that the proposal reaches results that even you yourself think are wrong. For instance, suppose that the proposal is

---

* *See, e.g.,* Jennifer E. Rothman, *Freedom of Speech and True Threats*, 25 Harv. J.L. & Pub. Pol'y 283, 336 (2001), for an example of one such test suite that the student used while writing her article, and eventually incorporated into the published version.

† The numbered notes in this book are endnotes, which you can read at p. 191. The endnotes generally contain supporting evidence for assertions in the text, or citations to other sources.

that religious objectors should always get exemptions from paternalistic laws. Thinking about test case 2 might lead you to conclude that people should not be allowed to help physically healthy people commit suicide. The proposed rule, then, would be unsound.

What can you do about this?

a. You might think that the proposal yielded the wrong result because it didn't take into account countervailing concerns that may be present in some cases—for instance, the special need to prevent a voluntarily assumed near-certainty of death or extremely grave injury, rather than just a remote risk of harm. If this is so, you could *modify* the proposed test, for instance by *limiting its scope* (for example, by adding an exception for harms that are likely to be immediate, grave, and irreversible).

b. Another possibility is that the insight that led you to suggest the proposal—in our example, the belief that there should be a religious exemption from peyote laws—is better explained by a *different rule*. For instance, as you think through the test cases, you might conclude that your real objection to the peyote ban is that it's factually unjustified (because peyote isn't that harmful), and not that it's paternalistic. You might then *substitute* a new rule: courts should allow religious exemptions from a law when they find that the religious practice doesn't cause any harm, whether or not the law is paternalistic.

2. *Vagueness:* You might find that the proposal is unacceptably vague. Say that the proposal was that religious objectors should be exempted from paternalistic laws when "the objectors' interest in practicing their religion outweighs the government's interest in protecting people against themselves." In the peyote case, this proposal might have satisfied you, because it was clear to you that the government's interest in protecting people against peyote abuse was weak. But as you apply the proposal to the other cases, you might find that the proposal provides far too little guidance to courts—and might therefore lead to results you think are wrong. This could be a signal for you to *clarify* the proposal.

3. *Surprise:* You might find that the proposal reaches a result that you at first think is wrong, but then realize is right. For instance, before applying the proposal to the test suite, you might have assumed that religious objectors shouldn't get exemptions from assisted suicide bans. But after you think more about this test case in light of your proposal, you might conclude that your intuition about assisted suicide was mistaken.

21

You should keep this finding in mind, and *discuss it in the article*: It may help you show the value of your claim, because it shows that the proposal yields counterintuitive but sound results.

4. *Confirmation:* You might find that the proposal precisely fits the results that you think are proper. This should make you more confident of the proposal's soundness; and it would also provide some examples that you can *use in the article* to illustrate the proposal's soundness (as Part I.B.3.c, p. 35, discusses).

c. Developing the test suite

How can you identify good items for your test suites? Here are a few suggestions:

1. *Identify what needs to be tested.* The test suite is supposed to test the proposed legal principle on which the claim is based. Sometimes, the claim is itself the principle: For instance, if the proposal is that "the proper rule for evaluating requests for religious exemptions from paternalistic laws is [such-and-such]," you would need a set of several cases to which this rule can be applied.

But sometimes the claim is just an application of the principle; for instance, the claim that "religious objectors should get exemptions from peyote laws" probably rests on a broader implicit principle that describes which exemption requests should be granted. If that's so, then you should come up with a set of cases that test this underlying principle. One case should involve peyote bans but the others shouldn't.

2. Each test case should be *plausible*: It should be the sort of situation that might actually happen. It's good to base it on a real incident, whether one drawn from a reported court decision or a newspaper article. You need not precisely follow the real incident, and you may assume slightly different facts if necessary—the goal is to have the reader acknowledge that the case *could* happen the way it's described, not that it necessarily has happened. But you should make sure that any alterations still leave the test case as realistic as possible.

3. The test suite should *include the famous precedents* in this field. This can help confirm for you and the readers that the proposal is consistent with those cases—or can help explain which famous cases would have to be reversed under the proposal.

4. At least some of the cases should be *challenging for the proposal*. You should identify cases where the proposal might lead to possibly unappealing results, and include them in the test suite. Skeptical readers, including your adviser, will think of these cases eventually. Identify-

ing the hard cases early—and, if necessary, revising the proposal in light of them—is better than having to confront them later, when changing the paper will require much more work.

5. The test cases should *differ from each other* in relevant ways, since their role is to provide as broad a test for the claim as possible. If you are testing a claim about paternalistic laws, for instance, you shouldn't just focus on various drug laws, or just on paternalistic laws aimed at protecting children. You should think of many different sorts of paternalistic laws, and choose one or two of each variety.

6. The cases should yield *different results*. For instance, if your proposed rule judges the constitutionality of a certain type of law, you should find some laws that you think should be found unconstitutional, some that you think should be found constitutional, and some whose constitutionality is a close question.

7. The cases should involve incidents or laws that appeal to as many *different political perspectives* as possible. Say that you are a liberal who wants to argue that the Free Speech Clause prohibits the government from funding viewpoint-based advocacy programs. You might have developed this view because you think the government shouldn't be allowed to fund anti-abortion advocacy, and your proposal will indeed reach the result you think is right in that case.

But what about advocacy programs that liberals might favor, such as pro-recycling advocacy, or advertising campaigns promoting tolerance of homosexuals? It would help if the test suite included such cases, plus generally popular programs such as anti-drug advertising, or programs that even small-government libertarians might like, such as advocacy of respect for property rights (for instance, anti-graffiti advocacy). This wide variety of test cases will help show you whether the proposal is indeed sound across the board, or whether even you yourself would, on reflection, oppose it.

d. Particular problems to watch out for

A proposal can be unsound in many ways, but a few ways are particularly common.

i. Excessive mushiness

Be willing to take a middle path, but beware of proposals that are so middle-of-the-road that they are indeterminate. For instance, if you're arguing that single-sex educational programs should be neither categorically legal nor categorically illegal, it might be a mistake to claim that such programs should be legal if they're "reasonable and fair, and promote the cause of justice." Such a test means only what the judge who applies it wants it to mean.

Few legal tests can produce mathematical certainty, but a test should be rigorous enough to give at least some guidance to decision-makers. Three tips for making tests clearer:

- Whenever you use terms such as "reasonable" or "fair," ask yourself what you think defines "reasonableness" or "fairness" in this particular context. Then try to substitute those specific definitions in place of the more general words.

- When you want to counsel "balancing," or urge courts to consider the "totality of the circumstances," ask yourself exactly what you mean. What should people look for when they're considering all the circumstances? How should they balance the various factors you identify? Making your recommendation more specific will probably make it more credible.

- If possible, tie your test to an existing body of doctrine, by using terms of art that have already been elaborated by prior cases (though this approach has its limits, as the next subsection discusses).

Thus, "single-sex educational programs should be legal if they have been shown in controlled studies to be more effective than co-ed programs" is probably a more defensible claim than "single-sex educational programs should be legal if they're reasonable." Instead of an abstract appeal to "reasonableness," the revised proposal refers to one specific definition of reasonableness—educational effectiveness—that seems to be particularly apt for decisions about education. It's still not a model of predictability, but it's better than just a "reasonableness" standard.*

Note how test suites can help you find and fix this problem. If you apply a proposal to your test cases, and find that it often doesn't give you any definite answer, you'll know the proposal is too vague. Once you discover this, you can ask yourself "what do I think the results in these cases should be, and why?" Answer this question, incorporate the answer into your original proposal, and you'll have a more concrete claim.

---

* Some people argue that very flexible tests are actually better than seemingly more rigid ones; if you share this view, you might reject my approach here. Remember, though, that many readers will rightly wor- ry about how your vague test will actually work out in practice. For your article to be convincing, you must either make the test more determinate or persuade these readers to accept its indeterminacy.

ii. Reliance on legal abstractions

"Reasonableness" at least sounds as vague as it is; other terms, such as "intermediate scrutiny," "strict scrutiny," "narrowly tailored," and "compelling state interest," seem clear but in reality have little meaning by themselves. To the extent that, say, strict scrutiny of content-based speech restrictions provides a relatively predictable test, the predictability comes from the body of caselaw that tells you which interests are compelling and what narrow tailoring means, and not from the phrase "narrowly tailored to a compelling state interest." The terms "strict scrutiny" and "narrowly tailored to a compelling state interest" aren't the test; they are just the names of the test.

Thus, a proposal such as "gun control laws should be examined to see if they are substantially related to an important government interest [i.e., intermediate scrutiny]" doesn't really mean much by itself. To be helpful, the proposal must explain which interests qualify as important and what constitutes a substantial relationship.

Nor is it enough just to say "the courts should borrow the intermediate scrutiny caselaw from other contexts." The intermediate scrutiny tests differ in different contexts, both on their face and as applied. Intermediate scrutiny in sex classification cases, for instance, has a reputation for being a very demanding test, while intermediate scrutiny of restrictions on expressive conduct has generally proven to be deferential; and if you look closely at the elements of the two tests, you'll find that they differ significantly, and for good reasons (since the underlying constitutional concerns animating the tests are different). Similarly, intermediate scrutiny in commercial speech cases was fairly deferential in the mid–1980s, but became much more demanding in the 1990s and early 2000s, all the while being called "intermediate scrutiny."

The solution is, in Justice Holmes's phrase, to "think things not words."[2] Rather than relying on words such as "substantially," "important," or "intermediate," explain which interests may justify the restriction and which may not. Explain when restrictions should be allowed to be overinclusive or underinclusive and when they may not be. Explain when courts should demand empirical evidence that the law serves its goals and when they can rely on intuition. Of course, you may not be able to cover all possible situations, and in some cases where the question is close, your test may properly leave things ambiguous. But the more concrete your proposal, the better.

Note again how test suites can help you identify this problem and refine your claim: Just as in the previous subsection, applying your proposed test to a set of concrete problems can help you see whether it has substance or is just words.

iii.   Procedural proposals that don't explain what substantive standards are to be applied

Procedural proposals can be useful: It's often impossible or politically impractical to design the right substantive rule up front, so the best we can do is set up the procedures that will make it more likely that the right rule will eventually emerge. The Constitution itself, for instance, was intended to protect liberty largely through procedural structures, such as bicameralism, separation of powers, and the like. If you genuinely think that the right answer to your problem is better procedures, you should propose that.

But remember that courts and administrative judges, unlike legislatures, are generally required to apply a substantive rule, even if a vague one. It's not enough just to set forth procedures through which these bodies act—if your proposal asks such entities to review something, it has to tell them what rule they should apply.

Thus, say that you want to limit speech restrictions imposed on students by K–12 school officials; but because you recognize that it's hard to have a clear rule establishing which restrictions are good and which are bad, you propose a statute that requires that any such restrictions be reviewed by administrative law judges. This might be a good solution, but you need to ask: What substantive test should these judges apply?

Your answer might be "the judges must make sure any restriction is constitutional"; but if that's so then you should make that clear—and you should also discuss whether such a proposal will indeed materially constrain school officials, given that the Constitution leaves them pretty broad authority over student speech (see *Tinker v. Des Moines Indep. Comm. School Dist.* (1969)). Alternatively, your answer might be "the judges should independently decide whether the restriction, on balance, is a good idea." Again, if that's your answer, you should make it clear, and discuss whether administrative judges will be good at making such educational policy decisions.

Or you might recognize that there *is* some implicit substantive rule that you want the administrative judges to apply, for instance, "political speech by students must be protected unless there is concrete evidence that the speech has actually disrupted classes." If that's so, you should make clear that your proposal isn't just about procedure but also about substance.

Likewise, it's often tempting to argue that courts should admit a certain class of evidence, for instance evidence about aspects of a person's cultural background that might have led him to act in a certain way. Why not let it in? Don't we trust jurors? Isn't more evidence better than less?

Well, maybe—but much depends on how we expect jurors to consider this evidence. Say that a defendant killed someone because the other person did something that the defendant's culture finds mortally insulting: the victim said something to the defendant, the victim pointed the soles of his feet at the defendant,[3] the victim made a homosexual advance to the defendant, or the victim, who was the defendant's wife, flirted with another man. And say that the defendant wants to introduce evidence of these cultural beliefs in his murder prosecution, seeking to have the jury convict him only of voluntary manslaughter, not murder.

Today, the presence of provocation can generally reduce the offense from murder to voluntary manslaughter only if the provocation is seen as reasonable by society at large. If this *substantive* rule is retained, then admitting the cultural evidence seems unwise, because jurors generally can't lawfully give effect to the evidence, and the evidence is thus more likely to be prejudicial or distracting rather than relevant.

Of course, if the substantive rule were changed to let murder be reduced to manslaughter whenever the defendant was provoked in a way that's seen as reasonable by the defendant's culture, then courts would have to admit evidence of what the defendant's culture actually believes. But this substantive proposal would be controversial, and should be defended explicitly. You can make your procedural proposal complete only by exposing the substantive assumptions behind it, or the substantive changes that would be required to make it work.

The same goes for proposals that:

- "courts should take a hard look at X" (a hard look applying what test?),

- "courts must carefully sift the facts" (what specific item will they be searching for in this sifting, and what role will this item play in what test?),

- "executive officials must state their reasons for action on the record" (and then their reasons would be reviewed for compliance with what rule?), or

27

- "there should be a hearing in which the affected parties may introduce evidence" (what legal rule would this evidence be relevant to?).

Focusing on procedure may often be good—but in such cases there's often an unexpressed substantive proposal lurking. Express it.

6. Selling This to Your Readers

Not only must your claim be novel, nonobvious, useful, and sound, but you must show your readers that this is so. More about this shortly (Part I.B.1.b, p. 31).

7. Topics and Structures You Should Generally Avoid

Here are some types of articles that you might want to avoid. These recommendations won't always apply: Sometimes, for instance, a journal may insist that you write a case note, or your article may deal with an important and interesting problem that arises only under one state's law. Nonetheless, I think that you'll find the suggestions below to be helpful in most situations.

a. Articles that show there's a problem but don't give a solution

Giving a solution makes your article more novel, nonobvious, and useful, and therefore more impressive. You want to show people that you have a creative legal mind that can identify solutions and not just criticize others' proposals. If you think there are several possible solutions, that's fine—just discuss all of them, and explain the strengths and weaknesses of each.

b. Case notes

An article that describes a single case and then critiques it is likely to be fairly obvious, even if it's novel and useful; and it generally doesn't show off your skills at research and at tying together threads from different contexts.

If you got your topic from a particular case, that's fine. But don't focus on the case—focus on the problem, and bring to bear all the cases that deal with the problem.

c. Single-state articles

Articles focusing on a single state's law are generally useful only to people in that state. Such articles may still be valuable, especially if the state is big; but why limit yourself this way?

Other states probably have similar laws, or might at least be considering them. Frame your article as a general discussion of all the laws of this sort, even if it focuses primarily on two or three states as representative cases.

Of course, the various state laws will probably differ subtly from each other, which may require some extra discussion. But while this means some more work, considering these differences may make the article more useful, sophisticated, nuanced, and impressive.

d. Articles that just explain what the law is

These can be useful, and sometimes even novel, but they tend to seem obvious. The reader is likely to say, "true, I didn't know this, but I could have figured it out if I had only done a bit of research." This is just fine if your reader is a busy lawyer looking for a good summary of the law—but not so good if the reader is a professor, a law review editor, or a judge looking for a creative, original-thinking law clerk.

There are exceptions: For instance, showing that the law is actually applied quite differently from the way most people assume might well be nonobvious. But even there, it would help to add a prescriptive component to your description. Should the law be applied this way? If not, how can the law be amended to prevent such applications? If yes, should the law be clarified or broadened to make such applications easier?

e. Responses to other people's works

Framing your article as a response to Professor Smith's article will usually limit your readership to people who have already read Smith's article, and will tend to make people see you (fairly or not) as a reactive thinker rather than a creative one.

If your piece was stimulated by your disagreement with Smith, no problem—just assert and prove your own claim, while demolishing Smith's arguments in the process. Cite Smith in the footnotes; Smith's opposition will help show that your claim is important and nonobvious. But don't let Smith be the main figure in your story.

29

f. Topics that the Supreme Court or the Congress is likely to visit shortly

You don't want to write an article that will be quickly preempted by a new federal statute or Supreme Court decision. At best, you'd then have to radically rework your article; at worst, you might have to throw it out altogether. If you're writing about the law of a particular state, then you likewise need to watch out for new statutes or high court decisions in that state.

Unfortunately, one common way that students find topics—by identifying circuit splits—involves a high risk of the article getting preempted. A circuit split happens when several federal circuit courts of appeals disagree on a particular question. That makes the question more worth writing about, because the split shows that there's an important problem with no obviously right answer. But a circuit split is also a signal to the Justices that it might be time for the Court to resolve the issue.

So if there's a circuit split on your problem, check to see how likely it is that the Court will consider the matter and thus preempt your work. First, make sure that, for each case involved in the split, the Court has denied certiorari or no petition has been filed and the time to file has run out. Second, ask the professors who work in the field whether they think it's likely that the Court will agree to hear a case on this subject soon. Third, ask the same question of the professors who specialize in the Supreme Court; they sometimes have a different perspective from those people who work on the particular subject area.

You might also do the same when there is no circuit split on the problem, but the problem seems likely to attract the Supreme Court's or Congress's interest for other reasons. Don't be paralyzed by the risk of preemption—the Court and Congress deal each year with only a small fraction of all the problems out there. But think a bit about how likely preemption seems to be.

Finally, do *not* write on a topic that you think the Court will resolve shortly, in the hope of getting your article published before the Court hears the case. True, it would be great if the litigants or the Justices read your article and relied on it—but that's highly unlikely. And once the Court acts, your article will be largely ignored, since scholars and lawyers will be looking for articles that consider the new decision, rather than articles that predate it.

B. *Organizing the Article*

1. Write the Introduction

A readable, interesting introduction is crucial to your article's success. Introductions have three important functions:

- (a) to persuade people to read further;
- (b) to summarize your basic claim for those who don't read further, so that they'll remember it and refer back to your piece when they run into a problem to which the claim may be relevant; and
- (c) to provide a frame through which those who do read further will interpret what follows.

To accomplish these goals, an introduction must do four things.

a. Show that there's a problem, and do this concretely

First, your introduction should make the reader think, "wow, I need to read the rest of this." The best way to get that reaction is to show that there's an important, interesting problem that needs to be solved. This could be a descriptive problem (does this law work? how did this legal rule come about?) or a prescriptive one (what should be done in these situations?). But whatever it is, you need to persuade readers that they should spend their time reading about this problem.

And the most compelling problems are *concrete* ones. Don't just say that the law is unjust or oppressive, or ignores transaction costs or the plight of the subordinated. Give a specific example—a real scenario is good, but a plausible hypothetical is fine too—that shows how the law can fail. Make the reader say, "interesting, it looks like the law here is unsound" or "I wonder what the right answer is."

This, of course, is related to demonstrating your claim's utility (see below), but it's important in its own right: It makes people want to read what you wrote.

b. State the claim

Second, you should briefly state the claim, and briefly show its novelty, nonobviousness, and utility. This tells the readers what to expect, and persuades them that your article will make a valuable original contribution by solving the problem as well as identifying it.

Note the "briefly." The introduction should be short, simple, and clear. It should make the reader want to read further, but it should also simply and memorably communicate your basic point—and the other interesting conclusions that you draw in the process of reaching it—even to those readers who will never read beyond the introduction.

The best way to show novelty and nonobviousness is implicitly, by briefly explaining your claim and justification in a way that makes the reader say, "I'd never have thought of that." But if you think people might wrongly assume that your topic has already been heavily discussed, and that your claim has already been made by someone else, you might explicitly say something like "surprisingly, it turns out that few scholars have considered [the question]."

Utility is also best shown implicitly; saying "this is a really useful point" will rarely add much to your argument. Instead, make sure that your introduction clearly summarizes your important findings, and their possible practical and theoretical implications.

c.   Frame the issue

Every law has many effects. In theory, readers' judgments about the law should be the same no matter how the question is presented, because in theory they should consider all the effects. But in practice, the frame—the way you present the issue to the readers—is important.

Consider an article about gun control. Thinking seriously about gun control requires thinking about many things: The thousands of people who die each year from gunshots. The plight of people who need a weapon to defend themselves against criminal attacks when the police aren't there to help. The special concerns of women, who tend to be physically less capable of defending themselves without guns, and who are victimized in particular ways by crime. The Second Amendment and state constitutional provisions that guarantee a right to keep and bear arms. The uncertainty about how useful guns are for self-defense. The uncertainty about how effective gun controls would be.

Your article will have to confront all these questions, but it matters a lot how you frame the discussion. If you start by stressing that there were almost 11,000 firearms homicides in the U.S. in 1999,[4] and return to this throughout the piece, the reader will be more likely to look at all the evidence through this lens. If you start by stressing that the police are often far away, and that hundreds of thousands or perhaps even millions of people use guns to defend themselves against criminal attacks each year, the reader may approach the evidence from a different perspective.

The introduction is the place where you construct this basic frame—where you give a simple summary that puts the reader in the right mindset to absorb and agree with your point. Write with this in mind.

d.   Do all this quickly and forcefully

The first few sentences of the introduction can make the reader drop the article, or keep reading it. Don't start with platitudes or generalities that the reader already knows. Start with something that is concrete, and that quickly communicates your perspective.

Consider, for instance, a draft introduction I once ran across:

> Campaign speech has long been a controversial topic among scholars and commentators. Much attention has been devoted to the Supreme Court's treatment of individual expenditures, contributions and spending in *Buckley v. Valeo*. Congress' recent consideration of campaign finance reform provides an ideal opportunity to revisit the 1976 Supreme Court decision that addressed the free speech implications of limits on federal campaign-related activities.

> This essay briefly discusses the effects of such limits on individual speech, the disproportionate treatment of speech by the media and justifications presented by several members of the Court in the 2000 decision, *Nixon v. Shrink Missouri Government PAC*.

> Let me begin by giving a concrete situation. Imagine you are outraged about a particular candidate's stand on something. [More concrete details follow, aimed at showing that there's a basic First Amendment right to spend money to express your views about candidates.] . . .

The first two sentences say something that's obvious to most readers, even those who barely know the field. The third and fourth sentences describe something less obvious—what the article's general topic will be—but they're clunky and boring. The fifth sentence likewise adds little.

It's only the sixth sentence—"Imagine you are outraged"—that has the power to grab the listener. It provides a concrete scenario, which is usually more interesting than generalizations. It also quickly sets the stage for the core argument, which is that you have a right to spend your money to express your views.

Start the introduction with this sentence, rather than hiding it after five sentences of generalities. If you need to make some general points, do it later, after you've gotten the reader hooked.

2. Explain Background Facts and Legal Doctrines

The purpose of your article is to state and prove your claim. That's where the action is, and you should be excited and impatient about getting there.

Before you get there, you'll probably have to describe some relevant background matters. If you want to write about why certain kinds of zoning laws violate the Takings Clause, you'll have to describe these laws briefly, and perhaps give a broad explanation of Takings Clause jurisprudence.

The key words here, though, are "briefly" and "background." Too many student articles spend eighty percent of their time summarizing the law and twenty percent explaining and proving their claims. Doing this is tempting: Summarizing the law is the easier task, and when you've spent many weeks doing research, it's hard to cut down the result to just a few pages.

But cut you must. Your claim and your proof are what you're adding to the field of knowledge; your achievement will be measured largely by this value added. You can't prove your claim without explaining the background facts and doctrine, but do this as tersely as possible.

Things to avoid, besides excessive detail:

a. *Summaries of each precedent in the doctrinal line*. Your job here is to synthesize the precedents, not to describe each one. Briefly state the relevant rule, in whatever detail is needed; cite your authorities in the footnotes. Do not say, "In *A v. B,* such-and-such happened. The Court ruled for A. Then in *C v. D,* the facts were such-and-such. The Court ruled for D. Then in *E v. F* ...." No one wants to slog through that.

If there's a leading case that you need to compare and contrast in detail with the scenario about which you're writing, you'll need to discuss the case in detail in the proof section. Don't repeat all this detail in the background explanation section.

b. *Minitreatises that go beyond what's needed to set the stage for your proof*. All you need to do in this section is give the reader the legal and factual framework necessary to generally understand what follows; you don't need to describe all the law and all the facts that you'll later use. You'll have plenty of time to go into more detail later, as you set out your proof.

c. *Unnecessary historical discussion*. If you want to say something about some area of law, you need to explain what the law is, but you don't necessarily have to go into much detail about how it came to be that way. If the history should affect our understanding of what the law means, you should of course mention it. But to the extent that the history doesn't matter, cut it out. Your main mission is to prove your claim. Unnecessary tangents might seem interesting and colorful, but in practice they usually end up being distractions and excuses for the reader to stop reading.

3.   Prove Your Claim

This is where you can shine, by showing that your claim is correct, and that it's the best way of solving the problem you've identified. Some tips:

a.   Show that your prescription is both doctrinally sound and good policy

Don't just show that your prescriptive proposal (if you have one) fits the case law; also persuade your reader that it's practically and morally sound. Authors often come up with a neat logical argument that supposedly proves a law's unconstitutionality or explains how a law must be interpreted, but that leaves many readers unpersuaded. To the extent possible, show that your proposal makes practical sense as well as logical sense—that it is good policy as well as consistent with the doctrine.

b.   Be concrete

Illustrate your theoretical arguments with concrete examples, drawn from real cases or realistic hypotheticals. This will make your point clearer to your reader; it will show that you have a point and aren't just playing a theoretical shell game; and it will often make your point clearer to you, or lead you to rethink it.

c.   Use the test suite

The test suite you used to show yourself that the prescriptive part of your claim is sound (see p. 19) can prove the same to your readers. The test suite involves concrete test cases. It illustrates different aspects of your proposal. And if done right, it involves cases that come from a variety of political perspectives, and thus shows that you've thought through a broad range of implications that your proposal may have, and not just those that seem to fit your politics.

At least in the first draft, try to mention every test case from your test suite.* Then, if necessary, you can remove the ones that prove redundant.

d.   Confront the other side's arguments, but focus on your own

Deal with all the counter-arguments, but take the offensive. Don't write "Some people say that this law fits within the captive audience doctrine, and this might at first seem plausible. Let me quote what they say: . . . . But on further reading it turns out that this isn't so, because . . . ."

Instead, write "the law can't be justified under the captive audience doctrine, because. . . ." Cite your adversaries and rebut their assertions, but don't let them be the main characters in your discussion.

e.   Turn the problems in your argument to your advantage

i.   Improve your argument

Squarely confront the logical and practical difficulties with your argument; don't try to sweep them under the rug. Be honest with your reader—it's the right thing to do, it's more effective, and it'll make you feel better about your work.

To begin with, confronting the difficulties can turn a banal, straightforward argument into one that's more nuanced and interesting. Say that the leading precedent in the field doesn't support your claim as squarely as you'd like. Don't just ignore this; explain how some other precedents or policy arguments fill the gap.

For instance, suppose your argument rests partly on the claim that public single-sex junior high schools are unconstitutional. You could just cite *Mississippi University for Women v. Hogan* and *United States v. Virginia* for your proposition, as some people do.

But these cases don't actually stand for quite so broad a principle—they involve college education, and they stress the particular characteristics of the programs involved in those cases. If you rely only on them, many readers will be unpersuaded, and you'll also have lost your chance to show off your reasoning skills. Rather, explain why the broader

---

*For examples of using test cases in a published article, see Eugene Volokh, *Freedom of Speech, Shielding Children, and Transcending Balancing*, 1997 SUP. CT. REV. 141, 183–87, and Jennifer E. Rothman, *Freedom of Speech and True Threats*, 25 HARV. J.L. & PUB. POL'Y 283, 336–66 (2001).

policies embodied in the Court's equal protection jurisprudence fill the gap between the precedents and your proposed rule; or explain why, even if a gap remains, your case is factually close to the situations in the precedents.

Do the same when you see ambiguity in the facts, history, statutory or constitutional text, or policy arguments: Acknowledge the ambiguity and explain why your choice is better than the alternatives. You shine by showing how you deal with the tough questions, not by pretending that the tough questions are easy.

ii.   Refine your claim

The difficulties can also lead you to make your claim more moderate and nuanced. Say your argument proves your claim in most cases, but not in all: For instance, say that it persuasively shows that single-sex K–12 schools are usually unconstitutional, but that it doesn't really work for programs specially aimed at students who have been sexually abused or who are mentally disturbed.

Maybe you should change your claim from "single-sex public education is unconstitutional" to "single-sex public education is generally unconstitutional, but single-sex public education of certain kinds of hard-to-teach children is constitutional." This may be a sounder claim, and it's also more likely to be novel and nonobvious.

iii.   Acknowledge uncertainty

The difficulties with your argument can also require you to acknowledge some uncertainty, and to prove your argument as best you can in the face of that uncertainty.

This can help make your work look more sensible and thoughtful. After all, little in our lives or in the law can be logically proven. We must often make the best guess we can, given gaps in the evidence. It's no great loss to admit this, assuming you have enough evidence to make your point plausible, even if not formally proven.

Say the cases are best read as holding only that public single-sex K–12 education is unconstitutional unless there's strong evidence that such programs are educationally valuable; and say people disagree about the evidence. Use the evidence on your side as best you can, acknowledge that there's disagreement, and make the best pragmatic, logical, and doctrinal argument you can for your point—for instance, you might argue that, in the face of disagreements about the facts, courts should err on the side of nondiscrimination and thus coeducation.

This is especially true for historical or empirical claims. It's hard to be sure about what people really believed or did many decades or centuries ago, or about what's happening in thousands of courtrooms or workplaces today; and readers who think deeply about such matters realize this. Make your descriptive claims clearly and forcefully, and explain why your interpretation of the history or of the data is the best one. But also acknowledge what other interpretations there might be.

iv. Acknowledge costs

Finally, the difficulties can make you acknowledge that your proposal is not cost-free: that it in some measure sacrifices some important government interests, or causes some possibly harmful side effects, or may at times be hard to administer. Skeptical readers will see these problems on their own, even if you don't admit that they exist. If you ignore the problems, the readers may assume the worst about the problems' magnitude.

If, however, you acknowledge the costs of your proposal but explain why the benefits exceed the costs, you can persuade many of the readers. No one expects any new proposal to be perfect. Explaining the proposal's downside can actually make it more credible—and can make you look more forthright and realistic.

4. Make Your Article Richer: Connect to Broader Issues, Parallel Issues, and Subsidiary Issues

a. Go beyond the basic claim

So far, we've focused on the core claim: The nugget of novelty, nonobviousness, and utility that will be your contribution to the state of legal knowledge. This is the heart of your article, and you should focus primarily on explaining and proving it.

Most claims, though, can provide insights that go beyond their narrowest boundaries; the claims have unexpected implications that flow naturally from them, even though these implications don't strictly need to be discussed. Exploring these matters can add nuance to your core claim that will make it more novel and nonobvious.

More broadly, it can make your article richer and more sophisticated—a thorough exploration of many facets of the problem, rather than just one narrow claim. Such an article will be more useful to people interested in the problem; and, if done right, these connections will make people think better of your article and therefore of you.

b. Connections: Importing from broader debates

Begin by asking yourself whether some of the issues you raise are special cases of broader matters on which there are already academic debates. For instance, if you are writing about a particular individual right, are there any theories of individual rights that you can draw on for your analysis? If you're interpreting one provision of a statute, is there a broader discussion going on in the law reviews about the statute's purpose or overall impact?

Say your work discusses whether a particular kind of statement should be admitted as evidence under some exception to the hearsay rule. There are many debates in the literature about hearsay generally—about whether hearsay should even be presumptively excluded in the first place, about whether there should be a single discretionary standard ("allow hearsay evidence if there are sufficient indicia of trustworthiness") or a relatively detailed rule with many detailed exceptions, and so on. Do some points raised in these debates help you support your arguments? Do they provide counterarguments to which you ought to respond?

These connections to broader matters aren't always helpful. Sometimes, the broader, more theoretical arguments are notorious for not giving much of a concrete answer in any particular case. In other situations, the broader discussion may be too many levels of abstraction above your particular question: If you're talking about whether certain disabilities imposed on felons violate the Ex Post Facto Clause, and if you already have lots of doctrine and policy argument to draw on for your analysis, a discussion of the debates about whether courts should rely on natural law or original meaning may not be terribly useful.

But sometimes the theories might indeed provide valuable insights. Even if their application won't form the core of your argument, they may shed light on a particular aspect of the argument, or supply important counterarguments that you should rebut. Also, discussing the theories can help assure the reader (a) that you aren't missing some theoretical objections, and (b) that you are a sophisticated thinker who knows the important theoretical literature. You shouldn't overdo this—a weak, unnecessary, or unoriginal application of the theory can sometimes alienate readers more than impress them. Still, if you can do a good job with the theory, your article will be more impressive.

c. Connections: Exporting to broader debates

Just as broad debates can have applications to narrower problems, good solutions to the narrower problems can illuminate a broader issue. If you have persuasively shown that the right answer here is X, and some broader theory says that the answer should be Y, then your concrete point is evidence that the broader theory is mistaken (or at least is not applicable here), and that the theory's rivals may be more sound. For instance, if you show that certain speech should be protected under the First Amendment even though under some free speech theory (the "marketplace of ideas," the "constitutional tension method," or what have you) the speech might be excluded from protection, then you might use your conclusion to cast doubt on the value of that theory more generally.

If done right, this sort of connection will make your piece deeper and more useful, and thus more impressive. People often accept or reject broad legal theories based not just on abstract legal arguments, but also on how well they fit with the results that seem proper in specific cases. Your article may provide powerful practical support or a powerful practical counterexample to some broad theoretical argument.

d. Connections: Importing from parallel areas

Sometimes, the best connections for your article come not from broader theories but from analogous issues in parallel areas. For instance, say that you are writing about whether waiting periods for buying a gun violate state constitutional right to keep and bear arms provisions.* Can you draw some analogies from the cases dealing with waiting periods for abortions, parade permits, or voting?

The analogies need not be perfect; you can often enrich your argument by pointing out the differences between your area and the other areas that at first might seem similar. Your reader might already have thought of these apparent similarities, and your discussion can dispel the reader's misconceptions. Likewise, the very process of pointing out the differences between, say, self-defense rights, abortion rights, speech rights, and voting rights might make the proof of your claim more persuasive. And sometimes, as with the importation from broader debates, the analogies may help you refine the claim itself.

---

* *See, e.g.,* WIS. CONST. art. I, § 25 (enacted 1998) ("The people have the right to keep and bear arms for security, defense, hunting, recreation or any other lawful purpose.").

e.   Connections: Exporting to parallel areas

Again, once you're done seeing what light the analogies from parallel areas can shed on your problem, you should ask whether your solution sheds light on the parallel questions. If you conclude that waiting periods for buying guns don't unduly burden self-defense rights, can you generalize to a broader claim about waiting periods for the exercise of other constitutional rights? If you think that the answer should be different in different situations, can you come up with a general principle that distinguishes contexts where waiting periods are undue burdens from contexts where they aren't? Or can you at least draw a distinction that can help differentiate the two kinds of contexts, even if it can't do the entire job itself?

Even if there isn't yet any broader academic debate on your general subject, your claim might have possible consequences that would be worth noting. For instance, your argument about one provision of a statute might illuminate the interpretation of other provisions; you don't need to analyze those provisions fully, but it helps if you at least highlight your argument's implications. Perhaps you can start a broader academic discussion yourself.

f.   Connections to subsidiary questions

Finally, consider what will happen if your claim is accepted. To begin with, ask what the people who would implement your proposed rule would have to do to make it work properly. Would prosecutors enforcing your proposed law have to exercise their discretion in unexpected ways? Would your substantive proposal have nonobvious procedural applications? Would there be problems of proof that might require changes to certain evidentiary rules, or at least to trial tactics? Discussing such questions can make your article more useful and complete, and might generate new and interesting insights.

For instance, say you're arguing that speech revealing certain facts about someone's sex life should be seen as tortious, and that liability for such speech wouldn't violate the First Amendment. Your substantive constitutional point can have procedural implications for how such trials should be conducted. For instance, you might argue that though compensatory damages should be allowed in such cases, punitive damages should be restricted, by analogy to the rule in certain libel cases. Or you might explore whether such speech should lead only to damage awards, or whether courts should also be allowed to enjoin the speech, despite the ostensible rule against prior restraints.

41

You might also find that in some contexts your claim has unexpected implications. For instance, does your broad point about revealing facts have particular consequences for publication of photographs, or of tape recordings? Even if the legal rule is the same, might it affect people's behavior differently in different situations?

Ask also what effect this rule will have on other tort rules. Will it make some of them unnecessary? Will it make others more important? For instance, in some recent cases the right of publicity has been used to bar the unauthorized distribution of nude photographs of celebrities. Would your proposed privacy right make such an extension of the right of publicity unnecessary or even undesirable?

g. A cautionary note

There are risks to exploring all of an article's implications:

1. If you explore them thoroughly, your article may become too long.

2. If you only sketch them lightly, the reader might find the discussion too cursory, too vague, or insufficiently supported; and this bad impression might undo some of the good impression that your core argument initially made.

3. If you don't structure the discussion right, some of the connections might become confusing tangents that distract your reader from the main point.

4. If you are too ambitious in looking for connections, you might find yourself drawing analogies that don't ring true.

The trick is to:

• create a solid core argument;

• incorporate into it those connections and implications that are necessary to a full understanding of your point;

• discuss the other connections and implications in some detail— perhaps in a separate section—while making clear that your main point doesn't stand or fall with them; and

• be cautious about the analogies you draw and the connections you make, and ruthlessly edit out those that on reflection don't seem persuasive enough.

Thus, first make sure that the readers understand your main point, and are impressed by it. Then, once they are already thinking well of you, they'll be more charitable towards any broader but tangential points that you might make.

But *be willing to cut those tangents*. Show readers—your faculty adviser, your trusted and thoughtful friends, your law review editor—a basically finished draft of your article. And if some of them tell you that some of the connections don't really work, be ready to edit them out.

Yes, it will be painful to jettison sections that you've worked hard to write, but you'll probably find that for every connection you cut, you'll be keeping two. And the connections that you keep will help make your article richer and more impressive than if you'd stuck only to the bare necessities.

5. Rewrite the Introduction

When you're done with your draft, rewrite the introduction. Since you wrote it, you might have:

(a) changed your claim,

(b) found better arguments for your claim,

(c) found better examples to illustrate your claim,

(d) found interesting and unexpected consequences of your claim,

or changed your thinking in other ways. Writing an article *should* change your thinking about the subject. Even if your bottom line remains pretty much the same, surely your understanding of the argument is now much deeper than when you started.

Rewrite the introduction using this newly acquired understanding. You'll find that the new introduction better fits the rest of the article, and that it better sells the article to the reader. In particular, make sure that you briefly mention all the important conclusions that the reader should take away from the article—not just your claim, but also the implications of the claim, such as those discussed in the last few pages.

Many readers will read only your introduction. Make sure that they get as much out of it as possible, both so they absorb more of your ideas, and so they have a higher opinion of you as a possible law clerk, colleague, co-counsel, consultant, or scholar.

6. The Conclusion

The conclusion is where you remind people of the value that your article has added to the debate. Briefly summarize your claim, and the most important subsidiary conclusions. But keep it quick—the reader is looking forward to being done.

C. *Converting Practical Work—Such as Law Firm Memos—Into Academic Articles*

Writing an article from scratch can be daunting. Fortunately, you can often save time and effort by adapting work you originally wrote for another purpose—for instance, for a summer law firm job or a judicial externship.

Not all such work can be turned into a good article; some lacks novelty or nonobviousness, the stress in the real world being largely on utility. But much practical work does focus on largely unexplored questions, as you might have found if you searched for relevant law review articles before starting to write. And though memos and motions are generally shorter and shallower than a good law review article, that can be remedied.

The trick is to ruthlessly strip away those things that are unsuitable for law review articles, and to add the material that you never included because it was unsuitable for practical work. I recommend a four-step approach: Extract, deepen, broaden, and connect.

1. Practical work often covers issues that were important to the case on which you were working, but that aren't new or academically interesting. *Extract* those portions that would be a valuable addition to the literature, and throw out the rest.

2. Practical work often glosses over counterarguments and omits significant steps in the analysis. *Deepen* it by confronting the hard questions that the original work avoided.

3. Practical work is generally tied to particular facts, a particular jurisdiction, or a particular procedural posture. Make it more useful by *broadening* your discussion.

4. Practical work tends to ignore (for good reasons) broader academic debates. Make your article more academically impressive and perhaps more useful to later scholars by *connecting* what you've written to these debates.

Ethical note: Before turning a law firm memo into an article, get permission from the firm. Most firms will want to make sure that you aren't inadvertently including confidential client material, but some might also not want you to share work that they paid for (and in which they own the copyright). Few articles are worth ruining your relationship with a prospective employer, or with a likely reference for future employment. Likewise with work you've done as a judicial extern or a law clerk.

If you're getting class credit for your work, you should also disclose to your adviser or seminar teacher that you want to base your paper on some material that you had written before. Some professors might balk at that, because they may think that you should only get credit for work that you've done specifically for school. That's the professor's prerogative, and you'll be glad that you checked with the professor up front, rather than having him learn this later, and accuse you of chicanery and of violating academic standards.

But other professors might recognize that turning a practical piece into an academic one itself requires a lot of work, and they would thus have no objection to your proposal—especially if you show them the original memo, with a brief but impressive discussion of the many things that you plan to do to it.

1. Extract

Find the material in your work that's novel and nonobvious. (Don't worry so much about utility; if the work was useful in one case, it will probably be useful in others like it.) Many cases involve some issues that have rather simple or at least not very interesting answers, and other issues that are more worthy of academic treatment.

Cut mercilessly. Remove any subtopics for which you think you can't really add any academic value. Don't worry if the result looks too short; you'll solve that problem in the next three steps. The important point is that your paper should contain maximum value added, and minimum repetition of what others have already said.

Some memos contain several interesting issues that arose in the same case but aren't inherently connected—for instance, a jurisdictional question and a largely unrelated substantive question. Split them up. Better to have several short articles, each of which has a coherent internal structure, than one long article that contains several essentially unrelated matters.

2. Deepen

Practical work encourages you to take certain shortcuts. Replacing these shortcuts with more thorough analysis will make your article deeper, more valuable, and more impressive.

a. Question existing law

If the case law in your state or your federal circuit is settled, your law firm memo or judicial externship bench memo generally isn't supposed to analyze whether the decisions are sound; it's supposed to work within the existing framework.

Not so for law review articles. Articles are generally addressed to a national audience, and other states or other circuits may be free to adopt a different rule. And an article may also argue that the Supreme Court, state supreme courts, or federal circuits sitting en banc should change even a settled rule—an argument that most practical memos rarely make.

So don't just say, "this result is right because *X v. Y* and *Z v. W* have so held." Instead say, "this result is right because it fits with these general principles (whether doctrinal principles or policy principles), and courts have indeed seen it this way (citing *X v. Y* and *Z v. W*)." Or feel free to say, "this result is right because it fits with these general principles; some courts have disagreed, but here is why they're wrong."

b. Take counterarguments seriously

Briefs often gloss over some counterarguments, whether because the counterarguments are so weak that they aren't worth discussing given the page limit, because they're so strong that the supervising lawyer prefers not to stress them, or because you think that this particular judge won't care much about them. Law review articles, on the other hand, are generally strengthened by a full discussion of the counterarguments.

Go through your work carefully and look for all the fudging. When you say, "because X is true, Y is true," is there a missing step? Is there a counterargument that you haven't confronted? Are you entirely persuaded by your own writing?

Resist the temptation to take the easy way out. Your article should aim to impress readers with your thoughtfulness and fair-mindedness; the best way to do that is to confront the hard counterarguments, not ignore them.

c. Reflect on your initial goal

Practical work is often constrained by its procedural posture. What should a prudent client do to avoid any chance of liability under a vague rule? What's the best place to file a particular case?

Ask yourself whether it's good that lawyers are asking these questions. For instance, maybe the legal rules shouldn't be so vague that they pressure people into taking the most conservative path; you could use the suggestions from your memo as illustrations of the rule's vagueness. Maybe the legal system should discourage forum-shopping in this context; you could use the discussion from your memo to show how the choice of forum makes a big difference.

Remember: You're no longer locked into the particular assignment you were given. You should take advantage of the time and effort you've invested in your work, but build on the work by thinking beyond the specific problem you were originally trying to solve.

3. Broaden

Practical work usually focuses on a particular fact pattern and a particular jurisdiction. While you want your article to be narrow enough to be manageable, you also want to make it more useful, and that means making it applicable to as many cases as possible.

You can often generalize your analysis with fairly little extra effort. Say your work dealt with only one state's law; usually the law in many other states will be similar. Turn your article into something that focuses on general U.S. law, or at least the majority (or even minority) rule.

You can still use the cases from your state as illustrations and as support for your argument. You'll need to do some more research on just how similar the law in the other states really is, but that tends to be considerably easier than researching a new subject from scratch.

Similarly, see to what extent you can easily generalize your fact pattern. Say your memo was about the remedies for unauthorized publication of the fact that someone is HIV-positive. You can probably broaden the work to cover unauthorized publication of the fact that someone has any medical condition that would lead some to shun him.

You might have to add a bit more analysis—there may be legally significant differences between HIV status and other medical conditions—but this may mean only a bit of extra work. Broadening the subject to "remedies for any unauthorized publication of private facts," however, would likely be much harder (and might therefore not be worth doing) because so much of your original analysis was likely to have been tied to your focus on a medical condition.

4. Connect

Finally, your work may profit from connections to debates in related areas (see p. 38), and these connections may even shed light on the proper outcome of those debates. Briefly but cogently discussing such connections can make your piece more useful and more impressive.

D. *Budgeting Your Time*

Students often find themselves running late on their papers, and as a result having to cut corners at the end of the semester. Try to avoid this by focusing up front on what you need to do, and when you need to finish it by.

Here's a sample plan and time-chart that you can use. (Some date boxes correspond to several steps, because those steps need to be done together.) Note that you should budget a *lot* of time—many weeks—for writing, and less time for research. The lion's share of the work is always in the writing.

Step	Target Completion Date
Identify a problem to be solved	
Create the test suite that you can use to test your claim	
Research: Read the articles that bear on the problem, to get an idea of what your claim should be, and to make sure that there's still something novel left for you to say	
Research: Read the cases, statutes, studies, and other original materials that bear on the problem	
Update the test suite to reflect new aspects of the problem that you found in your research	
Come up with a tentative claim	
Apply the claim to the test cases	
Refine the claim in light of the test cases	
Repeat the preceding three steps until you're satisfied	

Write the introduction	
Write the short summary of the background law; if you prefer, save this until after you write the proof of your claim	
Write the section that proves your claim	
Keep refining your claim as you write	
Write the conclusion	
Polish the writing and the structure (many editing passes)	
Rewrite the introduction to reflect the changes in your thinking, both about your claim and about how best to present it	
Hand in the first draft to your professor or to your law review Notes Department editor, and also to any friends who have agreed to help you with it	
Wait for readers' comments; while you're waiting, polish the writing, structure, and substance on your own	
Fix the substantive problems identified by readers (likely to be many)	
Polish the writing and structure in response to the readers' comments (several editing passes)	
Hand in the second draft	
Wait for the readers' comments; while you're waiting, polish the writing, structure, and substance on your own	
Fix the substantive problems identified by readers	
Fix the footnotes, fill in the citations that you originally omitted, find sources that you haven't yet found, and generally fill in all the blanks that you saved for later	
Polish the writing and the structure in response to the readers' comments (several editing passes)	
Update the introduction to reflect further changes in your thinking	
Hand in the final draft	

E. Deciding What to Set Aside

> "A poem is never finished, only abandoned."
>
> —Paul Valery

For many articles, there's no clear theoretical stopping point. You can always discuss other interesting legal issues that relate to your core

49

claim—for instance, if you're writing on a substantive free speech issue (e.g., the tension between the First Amendment and hostile work environment harassment law), you might see some interesting procedural questions that this raises: Should injunctions barring harassing speech be treated as prior restraints? Should there be independent appellate review in harassment cases that are based on speech?

Sometimes your running out of time or patience makes the decision for you. But if it doesn't, how do you know when to set these interesting points aside?

There's no clear answer to this, but my suggestion is to (1) thoroughly discuss your main claim, and then (2) have a short section that identifies and broadly outlines the other points, but doesn't fully resolve them. Generally, if you discuss your main claim in enough depth, you'll have a nice, substantial piece. Adding a thorough investigation of the tangents is unnecessary.

But flagging these tangents as interesting avenues for future research, and briefly giving some tentative thoughts on them, can help enrich your article and make it more relevant and useful. The very fact that your main topic raises these related questions can help show that the topic is important.

Make especially sure that you flag the implications of your claim, or of your framework for resolving the claim. These help show the importance not just of your topic (which existed before you started writing), but also of your analysis, which is your own contribution. If, for instance, you develop a test, briefly discuss where else the test, or tests like it, might be applied. If you develop a categorization scheme, briefly flag where else it could be helpfully used.

How brief should these tentative discussions be? That's a judgment call; you want them to persuade the reader that there's something interesting there, but you don't want them to get long enough that they make your article unnecessarily bulky and take up too much of your time. Four tips:

1. Ask your faculty adviser for advice, but *after* you've handed in the rough draft of your main discussion. Before you deliver the draft, the advisor won't be sure that you're able to handle even the core claim, much less the tangents.

2. Make clear at the start of the section that these points are avenues for future research, and that you will be discussing them only briefly. People's evaluations are related to their expectations: If they are warned that the discussion will be brief, they'll be less likely to be bothered by its brevity.

3. How substantive the digressions must be turns on how substantive your core argument is. If you deal thoroughly with your main claim, readers will be more likely to assume that your tangentially raised points are interesting, and that you would have dealt with them well if your article had been more focused on them.

4. Be prepared to delete these digressions—or to save them for a future article—if readers tell you that they're unpersuasive or distracting.

Finally, note that this has to do with how *broad* you make your article—how many related issues you choose to cover. If you have an opportunity to make your article *deeper*, by better justifying more of your arguments, do so (at least unless you think your justifications will be redundant). Inadequately supported assertions, or even assertions that are supported by the doctrine but not fully defended on policy grounds, make your argument weaker.

F. Choosing a Title

A title should do three things. Most importantly, the title should *persuade people to read the article*. When busy people do a WESTLAW or LEXIS search that yields fifty items, how do they choose what to read? They look at the authors' names and at the titles. If the title looks helpful—not necessarily exciting, but helpful—they'll read further. The title is your opportunity to get people to devote time to at least reading the Introduction.

Second, the title can *frame people's thinking* once they start reading your piece. If a title focuses the reader on a concept, the reader is more likely to keep that concept in mind.

Third, the title can *help readers remember your article*. Remember, though, that a memorable title is of little use to you if it wasn't attractive enough to get people to read the piece in the first place.

So how should you choose your title? Let me suggest the following approach.

1. *Start with a descriptive title*, which summarizes the general question that your article is answering (though not necessarily your

specific answer). If a person's query comes up with an article called "Freedom of Speech and Workplace Harassment," the person will have a good sense of the article's substance. Naturally, the title can capture only a small part of your point, but it can capture enough to give readers some idea of whether the article is relevant to their interests. Purely descriptive titles might not be that memorable, and might not much help frame readers' thinking, but they're good at getting people to read the piece.

Of course, it's not enough that your title be comprehensible to you; *make it comprehensible to your readers*. I named one of my articles "Test Suites," but late in the publication process realized that few readers would know what that means. Renaming the piece "Test Suites: A Tool for Improving Student Articles" made the purpose and value of the article clearer (though I think the title could have been made better still).

It's acceptable for an article to have *a subtitle as well as a title*. This can let you communicate two ideas, one general and one more specific. For instance, "Freedom of Speech and Information Privacy: The Troubling Implications of a Right to Stop Others from Speaking About You" conveys both a general point (the article is about the First Amendment problems with information privacy laws) and a specific one (the problems arise because "information privacy" really refers to a supposed right to stop others from speaking about you). The combination is long—perhaps too long—but it takes advantage of its length. Likewise, "Academic Legal Writing: Student Notes, Law Review Articles, and Seminar Papers" gives people a short summary (the book is about academic legal writing) but also tells them that it's useful for three different purposes.

2. *If your article focuses on a particular concept—and especially if it pioneers the concept—include the concept in your title.* Say you're writing an article about laws requiring passersby to help strangers whom they see to be in peril. Your main thesis is that these laws might have the perverse effect of *discouraging* some people from cooperating with the police; but you also think this broader idea of anticooperative effects of law deserves more attention in other contexts as well.

"Duties to Rescue and Anticooperative Effects of Law" may be a good title: It tells potential readers that your article is both about duties to rescue and about the general problem of law discouraging cooperation with the authorities; it focuses readers' attention on the concept of "anticooperative effects"; and it gives them a phrase that they can remember the article by. My colleague Ken Karst, for instance, pioneered the term "The Freedom of Intimate Association" in a *Yale Law Journal* article with that title, and now the phrase is a well-established part of constitutional jurisprudence.

3. *If you have a witty play on words that you'd like to include in the title,* now is the time to consider it. I try to avoid such titles in my own work, but I concede that a little wit can make the article seem more appealing, can put the reader in a good mood, and can help the reader remember the article later. I still remember an article title I saw in the early 1990s, "One Hundred Years of Privacy"—this both communicated the article's essence (a look back on the privacy tort a century after Warren and Brandeis first proposed it), and humorously alluded to the novel "One Hundred Years of Solitude."

But be careful! First, amateur comedians notoriously overestimate how funny their jokes are. Second, with some topics (abortion, the death penalty, and the like), some readers will find any humor to be jarring. Third, even an amusing gag distracts the reader from your main point. To be effective, the joke must be interesting and memorable enough that its value overcomes the distraction. So reread the title on several occasions to make sure that the gag really works, and ask friends whether they agree. If you're in doubt, err on the side of having a purely substantive title.

4. *Edit the title even more carefully than you edit the rest of your work.* Clarity, proper word choice, and liveliness are especially important in a title, both to make people more interested in reading the piece, and to set the right tone for their reading—if the title sounds clunky or abstract, people will expect the rest of the article to be the same. Thus, for instance, "Considering the Advantages and Disadvantages of Prohibitions on Concealable Firearms" isn't as good as "The Costs and Benefits of Handgun Prohibition." The "considering the" is surplus; "costs and benefits" is shorter and simpler-sounding than "advantages and disadvantages"; and "handgun prohibition" cuts out an unnecessary prepositional phrase, and recasts the abstract "concealable firearms" as the concrete "handguns."

5. *Generally, avoid case names.* Just as the article should usually be about a topic and not just a particular case (see Part I.A.7.b, p. 28), so should the title. First, the case name might not be familiar to some readers, unless the case is very famous; a reader might be interested in the general subject, but might not connect the case to the subject. Second, stressing a particular case makes your claim seem narrower and less useful.

Sometimes, a case may be so important and controversial that many readers will want to read articles about it—referring to the case name will then draw more readers than it will repel. But generally speaking, titles should be about concepts, not cases.

6. *Generally, avoid jargon, little-known legal terms, and statutory citations.* Readers may also be put off by titles with little-known legal terms, statutory citations (unless they're extremely well-known, such as "Title VII" or "42 U.S.C. § 1983"), and jargon, whether it's drawn from economics, literary criticism, feminist studies, libertarian philosophy, or what have you. Many readers will be interested in the general topic, but will not fully understand the terms; and when the query gives them those fifty titles, they'll choose the ones they understand rather than the ones they don't. Again, there may be exceptions, for instance if the substance of your article will only appeal to those people who know the jargon—then, the technical terms may attract exactly those readers that you want. But usually, stick with plain English.

7. *That other articles have silly or mystifying titles doesn't mean yours should, too.* Well-known authors can get away with less descriptive titles, since people will read their pieces because of the author's name, not the article's name. You don't have that luxury.

Here's an example. You decide to write an article about whether compulsory licensing of copyrighted musical compositions makes sense, using the recently decided *Allman v. Capricorn Records* as a starting point. Don't start with "Compulsion or Anti–Monopoly?" or "Licensing Fair and Foul," or, heaven forbid, "Copyright and § 115: Is *Capricorn* a Sign of the Times?"

Rather, (1) start with a descriptive title, such as "Copyright and Compulsory Licenses" or "Compulsory Licenses in Copyrighted Musical Compositions." These aren't exciting, but people who see the title will know whether the piece is likely to help them.

Then, (2) see if there are any other basic concepts around which your article is oriented. For instance, if you argue that compulsory licenses make copyright a form of "intellectual quasi-property," rather than true property, mention that concept in the title: "Compulsory Licenses in Copyrighted Musical Compositions: Intellectual Quasi–Property as a Remedy for Transaction Costs." This is especially so if you're trying to pioneer the concept of intellectual quasi-property.

If you do want to rework the title to (3) include some pun or witticism, now is the time to do it. This way, you have the descriptive title in front of you, and can compare it with the amusing alternative. If the amusing version is clearly better, go with it. But if it's not better— and it probably won't be better—then stick with the purely substantive title.

Now (4) see if you can make your title shorter, clearer, and more forceful. Does the subtitle really add enough value to the title? Do you really need the word "Compositions," or will the title be clear enough (and less technical-sounding) without it? Do you really need the word "Copyrighted," or will that be obvious, since virtually all musical compositions are protected by copyright? (I think "copyrighted" is probably helpful, because it makes it clearer to the casual reader that the article is about copyright law.) Can you make the title sound more active, perhaps "Compulsory Licenses in Copyrighted Music: Fighting Transaction Costs Through Intellectual Quasi–Property"? I'm not sure what the best title would be, but I am sure that you should spend some time editing it.

You don't have (5) any case names here, and you probably don't need them. "Transaction costs" is a bit of (6) economics jargon, but it's so well-known that it's probably worth keeping, especially since there's no really good synonym. You don't have any technical legal terms or statutory cites, which is good: If your title had been "17 U.S.C. § 115: Fighting Transaction Costs Through Intellectual Quasi–Property," you should have changed it to our working title ("Compulsory Licenses . . .")—many readers, even ones who know something about copyright law, might not be sure what § 115 covers.

So you now have a pretty good title. It's not very exciting, but it should get the job done. Someone who is interested in compulsory licenses and who comes across a piece labeled "Compulsory Licenses in Copyrighted Music: Fighting Transaction Costs Through Intellectual Quasi–Property" will probably think it's worth looking at—and that's the title's main function.

G. Summary

1. Choose a Topic

Choose an area that you find interesting, and that your faculty adviser thinks is a fertile ground for novel, nonobvious, and useful ideas. Find a problem in that area. Do research to learn more about the problem, and to figure out the possible solutions. Be open to switching to another problem if your research leads you to something more interesting or productive.

2. Make a Claim

Figure out what claim you want to make—what you think is the best solution to your problem. Formulate it in one or two sentences. If your claim is prescriptive, design a test suite based on the factual scenarios that you've identified in your preliminary thinking, and refine the claim in light of what you learn from applying it to your test cases. Use the pointers in Part I.A to make the claim more novel, nonobvious, and useful.

Do your research (see Part III). Modify your claim in light of your research. Try to make your revised claim still more novel, nonobvious, and useful.

3. Write a First Draft

Write an introduction. If you can't do that, you're probably not ready to write the draft—you're probably not yet sure what you want to say or how you want to say it. Look over Part I.B.1 for some pointers.

When you're done with the introduction, write the rest of the article. In this phase, don't stop when you find yourself blocked on one section. Just get a draft out, even if it's rough and incomplete in spots. As you write, be open to revising your claim further.

Rewrite your introduction in light of what you've learned while writing the draft. Try to enrich your article by discussing connections to related issues.

4. Edit

Go through as many drafts as you can, polishing each paragraph, each sentence, and each word. Look over Part IV for some pointers.

Also go back over Parts I.A and I.B.4. Can you make the piece more novel, more nonobvious, and more useful? Can you tighten up its organization? Can you sell it better in your introduction? Can you add further interesting connections?

At some point in the editing process—preferably as early in the semester as possible—give a draft to your faculty adviser for comments. Also ask for comments from some friends whose judgment you trust. Don't wait on this until it's too late.

5. Publish and Publicize

See Part VII.

6.   Think About Your Next Article

See Part VII.E.

*

II. SEMINAR TERM PAPERS

A. *Introduction: Comparing Seminar Term Papers and Academic Articles*

Seminar term papers are often much like law review articles, though the rules vary from instructor to instructor.

1. Nonobviousness

Seminar term papers should be nonobvious. Your goal is to impress the professor with your smarts and your creative thinking. Papers that apply settled law or well-established arguments to slightly new fact patterns generally won't serve this goal, and won't get a good grade.

2. Soundness

Seminar term papers should of course be sound; and your instructor, who specializes in the seminar topic, will be a much more critical judge of the quality of your arguments than a casual reader of an article would be.

3. Writing and Structure

Seminar term papers should be well-written and well-organized. True, you have a captive audience, and needn't worry that a boring introduction will lose the reader. But most instructors see the seminar paper as a way of teaching you how to write better, and they will therefore prefer that your paper be as engaging as possible. Likewise, though some professors might let you omit some sections—such as the discussion of the background legal rules—others might see the paper as an opportunity for you to practice writing sections like this, and will therefore insist that they be done well.

4. Utility

Utility may be less necessary, depending on what your professor prefers. As Part I.A.4 pointed out, utility is a relative matter: The goal is to make the work as useful as possible given your area of interest. Not every work needs to appeal to thousands of lawyers, but once you choose a topic, you should do what it takes to make your work appeal to as many readers as possible.

In a seminar paper, the instructor may relax this constraint, since the work will have exactly one reader. Still, some instructors may insist on utility even there, because they want you to use this opportunity to learn the skill of making articles more useful.

5. Novelty

Novelty may also be less necessary, depending on what your professor prefers. Because the paper isn't meant to be published, your teacher might conclude that your paper doesn't have to say something that's genuinely new to those who work in the field. It may be enough that it say something that is new *to you*, and that shows that you've thought about the matter yourself.

Many instructors, though, prefer that seminar papers be novel. First, seminars are supposed to teach you to think creatively and originally—to come up with ideas that others haven't had.

Second, if your paper does say something that someone else has already said, the instructor might suspect that you didn't really do that much work on it yourself, but just relied, consciously or not, on the arguments of others. He might not think you were plagiarizing; you might have properly given credit to people, and cast everything in your own words. But he might feel that your work may not have involved as much hard thinking as a more novel proposal would require.

Finally, novel work is just more impressive—it better shows off your abilities. Even people who say they don't require novelty will often value a novel paper (all other things being equal) more than a paper that says what many others have said before.

B. *Figuring Out What Your Instructor Expects*

As you see, while most seminar papers have the same general requirements, different instructors do things differently. Your first task, then, is to ask about what your instructor expects. Does the instructor want the work to be novel (again, in the sense of novel to scholars, as opposed to just novel to you)? Does the instructor expect it to summarize the background legal principles, as well as setting forth a new proposal? Does the instructor prefer that you spend more time describing the law (to show that you've learned the subject matter well), instead of setting forth any suggested changes? Will the instructor give more credit for a topic that's designed to be as useful as possible to its fictional readers?

Many instructors will quickly give you and your classmates clear guidance on this. A few, though, might not have thought fully about the matter, which is why asking them for specifics can be helpful.

You're writing *for an audience of one*. Start by figuring out what that person expects.

C.   *Finding a Topic*

Topics for seminar papers are generally limited to the seminar's subject matter. Sometimes this limitation can be helpful: I suspect that many students struggle a long time to find a topic for a publishable article precisely because there are so many fields to choose from.

Here are a few tips:

1. *Use the teacher.* Ask your professor to recommend some possible topics. Some teachers don't like to provide paper topics, since they think that finding a topic is part of the student's task; but others are more accommodating. Professors usually teach seminars in subjects that they like, that they write about, and that they read about. They therefore often have many topic ideas.

2. *Use the readings.* In most seminars, you end up reading recent academic papers. See what topics are flagged as unresolved by the readings, or are glossed over with only a shallow analysis. Don't frame your paper as a response to the particular article (see p. 29) unless your instructor tells you that this is fine. Organize it instead around the issue that you've identified from the readings.

3. *Use the discussions.* Listen carefully during class discussions. If classmates are debating a particular question and you see there's no clear answer, the question might be worth exploring further. Check with the instructor when you've identified such a topic, since you might end up using some insights that were first raised by classmates; but generally the instructor won't mind, because your written analysis of the subject will require vastly more thinking than the classmates' off-the-cuff statements did.

4. *Use the news.* Many seminar readings and class discussions mention recent events, which often contain the seed of an interesting article. Don't feel constrained by the circumstances of a particular event, which may raise only a very narrow question, or have some unusual aspects. Use the event as a concrete example that helps you identify and confront a broader problem.

D. Budgeting Your Time

Students often have less time to write a seminar paper than a student article. Student article topics, and especially law review Note topics, tend to be chosen during the summer or at the start of the semester. In a seminar, though, you may have to wait until mid-semester, after you've gotten into the material and perhaps gained a better sense of what you want to write about.

This makes it especially important to manage your time wisely. You need to have the time to select a topic, do your research, write several drafts, and (if the instructor allows it) have your instructor read and comment on at least one draft. So look at the timeline on pp. 48–49, adjust it for your seminar's timetable, and stick to it.

E. Turning the Paper into a Publishable Article

Once you've written a seminar term paper, publish it. You've done the work; why not get an extra credential out of it?

Don't worry if you aren't on law review. If your paper is any good, you can get it published in some outside journal (see Part VII.A, p. 137). And while you might not get into the most prestigious law reviews, a publication in a specialty journal or a second-tier journal is better than no publication.

You'll probably need to do some extra work to make the paper publishable. For instance, if your instructor let you skip explaining the legal background, you might need to fill in that section. But generally this isn't hard, since you've already thought through the problem, done the research, and written the paper. Even a law firm memo can be turned into a law review article (see p. 44), though the two are very different genres. A seminar paper is much closer to an article already.

Obviously, if you're planning to do this, ask your professor for advice: He might have suggestions that he never mentioned when the discussion was focused only on your writing a student paper. Better still, if you plan from the beginning to turn the seminar paper into an article, talk to your professor about this up front. He may have ideas about your choice of a claim and your organization that he wouldn't have mentioned had he not been thinking about the paper eventually becoming publishable.

III. RESEARCH

You should come to your writing project generally understanding how to find cases, statutes, and law review articles that deal with a given topic; your first-year research class must surely have taken care of that. I'll therefore just provide some extra tips that I think are particularly useful when writing articles and seminar papers.

A. *Identifying Sample Cases and Incidents*

Part I.A.1.c, p. 11, discusses ways you can identify an interesting topic to write on. Some of these ways will themselves point you to one or two cases that show how the topic arises in real life.

Look closely at these cases, and find more like them. Such sample cases:

1. help you figure out what you think about the problem,

2. introduce you to the arguments that have been made by the judges and lawyers in those cases,

3. show you what related problems your topic might implicate,

4. help you make the topic concrete for readers,

5. help you persuade readers that there really is a problem that needs to be solved, and

6. form the kernel of the test suite that you'll use in designing your claim (see p. 19).

Generally, the more different examples you have to start with, the better.

How do you find more examples? Here are a few tips:

1. Look for cases that your initial cases cite.

2. Look for cases that cite your initial cases.

3. Search for some of the keywords that are likely to be present in cases that implicate your topic. If those keywords are likely to find too many cases that are only tangentially related to your problem, limit your WESTLAW search by using the SYNOPSIS field—for instance, "SY(COPYRIGHT & PARODY)" will find all cases that have the words "copyright" and "parody" in the case's

synopsis, not just anywhere in the text. LEXIS's OVERVIEW field will also work for this.

4. Look for administrative agency decisions that involve this issue. In many fields (for instance, public accommodation discrimination law), cases are often filed before federal, state, or local agencies, and then aren't appealed to a court. Some such agency decisions are available on WESTLAW and LEXIS, though you'll have to search each agency's decisions separately; there's no "all administrative agency" database that you can use. Find the relevant WESTLAW and LEXIS databases (in WESTLAW, the IDEN database helps you find other databases), and look through them.

5. Look for attorney general opinions (in WESTLAW, AG and USAG, and in LEXIS, STATES;ALLAG) that deal with your topic.

6. Look for newspaper or magazine articles that discuss incidents that might never have turned into an electronically available court decision.

7. Do an Internet search (for instance, using google.com) to find other incidents.

8. Look through legislative history databases to see whether any statutes might have been proposed to deal with your problem.

B.   Understanding the Law

1.   Get the Big Picture

Once you've identified your general topic, figure out the general structure of the applicable legal regime. For instance, if you plan to write on free speech and captive audiences, learn the structure of free speech law. If you plan to write on the copyrightability of clothing designs, learn the structure of copyright law.

Start by *reading a short book* that's aimed at introducing students or lawyers to the field. Books in Foundation's Concepts and Insights series, West's Nutshell series, and Matthew Bender's Understanding series are often good for this. Ask both a reference librarian and the professors who teach in the field to recommend the book that they think is the best.

Do this reading even if you've done well in a class on the subject. First, you might have forgotten some important details. Second, few classes cover the whole field; they omit many topics, some of which may be important to your problem.

Much of the book, of course, won't directly relate to your particular question. But some of it will, and you might not know in advance which parts will and which won't.

For instance, if you're writing on free speech and captive audiences, you don't just need to understand the cases that have mentioned captive audiences. It turns out that you also need to know at least:

(a) the distinction between content-based restrictions and content-neutral ones,

(b) the distinction between the government acting as sovereign and the government acting as proprietor or K–12 educator,

(c) the distinction between commercial speech restrictions and other restrictions,

(d) the obscenity cases that discuss the risk that some people will inadvertently see the offensive material,

(e) the cases elaborating the meaning of "strict scrutiny" in free speech law, many of which happen to be campaign finance cases,

(f) the rules dealing with offensive speech generally, and

(g) various free speech procedural rules, such as the void-for-vagueness doctrine and the overbreadth doctrine.

Moreover, to make the policy arguments needed to support your claim, you may have to draw on principles that arise even in doctrinally unrelated areas. Captive audience questions, for instance, have little to do with incitement law and libel law. But when you write about captive audiences, you'll probably need to discuss arguments about the marketplace of ideas, chilling effects, and the like—and you'll want to draw analogies to the way those arguments have been made in leading incitement and libel cases.

2. Get the Details

After you broadly understand the general area in which you'll be writing, you need to learn about the specific topic in much more detail.

a. Start with *a treatise*. Read carefully the chapter that discusses your topic, plus any other chapters that you've identified as doctrinally connected to your topic. Pay close attention to the footnotes, pocket parts, and other updates.

If there are multiple treatises, find the best one by asking your librarian or the professors who teach in this field. In some fields, different treatises are known for having particular ideologies; if this is true of your field, read the best treatise on each side.

b. After you're done reading the treatise chapters, go back and see which cases and statutory sections seemed to be the most important; then *read each entire case and statutory provision carefully*, from beginning to end.

Treatises usually tersely summarize most cases, and often omit important policy arguments, implicit limitations, and even significant doctrinal details. And while a treatise will usually give you a good sense of the broader legal context, sometimes it will omit some context that is irrelevant to most lawyers but quite relevant to your argument. There's thus no substitute for reading the cases and statutes themselves.

3. Find Other Works on the Topic (the Literature Search)

Once you get a sense of what the law is, you need to find the important articles and books that touch on your particular topic. You should read them because (1) they might say something useful, and (2) you need a novel claim (or at least a novel argument for your claim), so you need to know what has already been said.

How can you find these works? First, *check the Index to Legal Periodicals and the Legal Resource Index* (available in WESTLAW as the ILP and LRI databases), and of course the book catalog in your law library.

Second, for many topics there are several cases that are so important that any serious article on the subject must discuss them. *Search for all the articles that mention those cases*. If that yields too many articles, try doing an ATLEAST search in LEXIS, finding all articles that mention the cases at least a certain number of times. Do the ATLEAST search using the case's short-form name, since an article may cite a case fully only once and then use the short form.

Third, ask your professor and others who teach in the field for the titles of articles *or names of authors* that you should check out. People will often forget particular titles, but remember the authors who are working on the subject. Use professors' suggestions, though, only as starting points: Few scholars know everything written in the field, so you need to do your own research to make sure that you don't choose something that has been preempted.

C. *Knowing When to Shift from Research to Writing*

When exactly are you done with your research? It's impossible to tell for sure: There's always the risk that you haven't found some key case or some perfect example.

Realize, though, that starting writing doesn't mean stopping your research—it just means shifting your primary energies to writing. While you're writing, you'll find yourself supplementing your initial research as you realize that your original searches didn't address some important aspects of the problem. And this extra research might well have been impossible at the outset, because you didn't know that it was needed until you really thought through the question, and you couldn't really think through the question until you had to write down your answer. Your understanding of the caselaw and the factual background doesn't have to be perfect when you start writing. It's enough if you understand the basics, and fill in the gaps later.

As Pam Samuelson has pointed out, the trick here is to know yourself.[5] Many of us (including me) use research as a device for procrastinating, because research is more manageable and less daunting than writing. If you fall into this category, force yourself to shift to the writing phase earlier than you normally would. Conversely, if you've found that you tend to breeze through the research, then do a bit more than you usually do.

*

IV. WRITING

This short chapter is surely no substitute for years of learning to write well, and for your first-year writing class. Still, here are some items that I've found to be particularly relevant to academic writing.

A. *There Are No Lazy Readers—Only Busy Readers*

Many writing tips stress simplicity, clarity, and brevity. Avoid unnecessary long words and complex sentences. Get to the point quickly. Keep paragraphs short. Make things easier for your readers, and keep them from losing interest.

Some writers think this advice assumes that readers are lazy or stupid; those writers feel they're being told to "dumb down" their prose for dumb readers. After all, smart, industrious readers wouldn't mind long paragraphs filled with long sentences and long words—they would focus on the substance, not the form.

No. Your industrious and smart readers are busy people, precisely because they are so industrious and smart. They can spend only limited time and effort reading your article—not because they're lazy or dumb, but because they have other things to do.

They can parse complex words and sentences; but this parsing takes more work than reading simpler, clearer prose. Why waste my time wading through this morass, they'll ask themselves, when I could be working on something else? You can keep their precious attention only by making things as easy for them as possible.

B. *Go Through Many Drafts*

"Nothing is ever written," my high school journalism teacher taught us; "it is rewritten."* Aim to produce your first draft well before the deadline. This is hard, but critical.

Print the draft, edit it thoroughly, and enter the changes. Edit the draft on the printout, not on the computer; it's generally easier to spot errors that way. Set the draft aside for a day if you have the time, or for a few hours if you don't have a day. Repeat often.

Even with my writing experience, I try to do about 10 complete edits before sending an article to the law reviews. When I clerked for Judge

* Giles K. Chesterton, Beverly Hills High
School.

69

Kozinski, the norm was about 30 to 40 drafts for an opinion, which included 20 to 30 substantive edits (the others were primarily cite-checks). Balzac supposedly went through 27 drafts of one book—and without a word processor.[6]

This is painful and time-consuming, but necessary. Your first draft will be badly flawed, unless you're a great writer, in which case it will be merely mediocre. So will the second through the fifth. As you're editing, keep some old drafts, and compare the tenth draft against the first. You will notice a vast difference.

C. If You See No Red Marks on a Paragraph, Go over It Again

At least during the first few drafts, every paragraph—even every sentence—will likely need to be corrected, made clearer, and made more forceful. If you're not seeing at least one flaw in each paragraph, you're not looking hard enough.

D. If You Need To Reread Something To Understand It, Rewrite It

As you're reading your draft, watch for times when you find yourself rereading a sentence or a paragraph. If your writing confuses even you, won't your readers be still more confused? And a reader who finds it hard to understand your writing will often stop reading.

"But this is complicated material," you might say. That may be right—but your job is to make the material as clear and as simple as possible. And a clear explanation should be readable in one pass: Remember, your readers aren't lazy, but they are busy.

E. Read the Draft With "New Eyes"*

As you read any assertion you make, ask yourself what a skeptical reader—not a sympathetic one—would say. The changes you make to satisfy this reader will enrich your argument for all readers.

Of course, this advice is easy to give but hard to follow. A few tips:

1. *For every sentence in your argument, ask "why?"* Say that your sentence is "this result would be undemocratic"; ask yourself

---

* I owe this expression to Judge Kozinski.

"why is this so?" Either the sentence itself or the sentences that precede it or follow it must answer that question (unless the answer is obvious). If you don't see the answer there, put it in.

2. *For every sentence in your argument, ask "why not?"* For the same sentence, ask "why might a reasonable person think the opposite?" Might there be several possible definitions of what is "democratic"? Might there be reasons to doubt the accuracy of the assumptions that lead you to your conclusion? If you can think of a plausible counterargument, make sure you address it.

3. *Imagine someone whom you respect but who takes the opposite view from you*—a friend, a professor, a judge—and try to read the piece as if you were that person. What counterarguments would he come up with? Would he be impressed by your logic, or would he see some flaws with it?

4. *Get a classmate to read the draft.* The classmate must be (a) smart, (b) willing to read the piece carefully, and (c) willing to give criticism, even harsh criticism. Of course, those who like you enough to satisfy criterion (b) may be less likely to satisfy criterion (c); people who satisfy all three criteria are rare and valuable. Buy them dinner as compensation. (Warning: Check first to make sure that your professor doesn't have any objection to others reading your draft. Most professors won't, at least for your articles and probably even for your seminar papers; but it's always good to check.)

5. If you have the time, *put your latest draft away for a day or two* before rereading it, so you can come back to it with a fresh perspective.

6. *Conquer your fear.* It's natural to be afraid of reading your own work critically. What if your claims are all wrong? What if you find the killer counterargument? What if you have to start over?

   The fear is understandable, but nearly always unfounded. If your claim is flawed, you can correct it. Most counterarguments are answerable, and if you find one that isn't, you can amend your claim without throwing everything out. Your draft represents a lot of research and thinking. Even if you have to revise it dramatically, you'll still be able to use the bulk of what you've written.

   And if you figure out that your claim is wrong, then your readers—including those who will grade your work—will too. Better fix the claim before you turn in the article.

F. Finish the First Draft Quickly/Defeat Writer's Block by Skipping Around

Sit down and write the first draft. When you get blocked on one section, go on to the next. If you need to leave a subsection for later, that's fine. If you feel that the best you can do is outline a section, or write a few unconnected paragraphs, do that.

Just keep going forward, and don't let your difficulties with one part interrupt the whole writing project. Usually, even if you're bored with one section or confused about what you want to say, you'll be invigorated by moving to another part of your argument. And once you have the first draft done, no matter how rough it is, revising it and filling the gaps will probably be much easier.

Your producing a first draft quickly, and then quickly improving and completing it, will also give your faculty adviser more time to give you useful feedback, and maybe to read through more drafts; and it will make you look industrious and disciplined—which is how you want the person who's grading your work to see you.

G. React Effectively to Your Professor's (and Other Editors') Suggestions

Once you've gone through several drafts, your professor may be willing to read your work and give you advice. Different professors operate differently: Some may be reluctant to read any rough drafts, especially for seminar papers, while others will be willing to read at least one such draft, or even more. Some may give you only general comments about the substance, while others may also edit your writing, at least in one or two sections. A few suggestions:

1. *Ask the professor up front* (a) whether he will read over a rough draft, and also (b) whether he will give you suggestions about your writing as well as about the substance. Sometimes, if you ask nicely enough—in a way that makes it clear that you really want to improve your writing—the professor will agree to more than he might have otherwise offered.

2. *Give the professor a draft that you've already closely proofread.* First, you want the professor to identify the problems that you wouldn't have found on your own—the problems that remain after several edits that you yourself did. Second, badly written prose is hard to read, and the harder the draft is to read, the less

closely the professor will read it. Third, the professor may feel that you're wasting his time by asking for comments on material that you haven't already edited yourself. You don't want your editor, or your future grader, to think that.

3. *Give the draft to the professor as early as possible.* This is in some tension with #2, but you need to keep both goals in mind. It will take time for the professor to read your draft and give you thorough comments—and this won't be the only task on the professor's schedule. The earlier you hand in the draft, the earlier you'll get the feedback, the more time you'll have to react to it, and the easier it will be for you to persuade your professor to read another draft. And you don't want the professor to feel rushed, because that will yield less thorough comments.

These points are fairly obvious, but here's one that many people forget:

4. *Treat each editing comment as a global suggestion, not just a local one.* If the professor circles one "it's" and tells you that it should be an "its," check *all* the "it's" in your paper—you've probably made this mistake more than once.

   Do the same for broader comments. Professors reasonably assume that once you see a few sentences marked "redundant" or a few paragraphs marked "too long," you'll understand that your prose needs trimming. They might not take the time to mark all the other instances of these problems.

   So as you read the marked-up draft, keep a checklist of the kinds of problems that the professor found. Then, focus your next edit on identifying and correcting more examples of each problem.

H. *Use Section Headings and a Table of Contents to Help Organize Your Thinking*

Readers find subsection headings helpful: Even if your article is well organized, readers might at times lose sight of the structure, and subsection headings can bring the reader back on track. Try to choose headings that refer to your specific argument (such as "Identifying Speech That Lacks Value When Communicated to Minors"), rather than generic ones such as "Background" or "Applying the Test."[7] Subsection breaks also provide extra white space on the page, which seems to make text more appealing to many readers.

But the main value of these subsection breaks is to help you organize your own thinking. If you break up a section into five subsections, giving each a topical heading, you'll be more likely to see organizational problems, such as shifts from one issue to another and then back to the first, or digressions that break up the article's logical flow.

Naturally, there will be some overlap among the subsections within each section. But to the extent possible, you should completely cover each detail within a few adjacent pages, rather than returning to it repeatedly throughout various parts of the article. Readers find it hard to grasp an argument that's made in five chunks in five parts of the paper. They'll need to do this for your broad argument, which will indeed pervade the whole article. Don't ask them to do the same for the more detailed arguments.

Good places for subsection breaks are usually easy to spot. For instance, when you're dealing with a multi-prong test, it generally makes sense to have a subsection for each prong, even for a prong that takes only several paragraphs. Many multi-pronged tests actually have several subprongs contained within each prong; consider having a subsection for each of these subprongs. Be willing to have subsections that go four or five levels deep.

If you're discussing several factual scenarios, policy arguments, or statutory sections, consider having a separate subsection for each one. Err on the side of having more subsection breaks rather than fewer.

After you're finished, you might decide to delete some of the lower-level subsection headings, especially if the subsections are very short, and the structure of the broader section is clear. Still, the headings will have served the goal of helping you write the article, even if they won't be needed to help the reader read it.

Most word processors can easily produce a table of contents from your section headings. Use this feature, partly to help the reader, but mostly to give you an overview of the article's structure as the headers reflect it. The table of contents may help show you some missing steps, or some redundancies.

The table of contents can also point out inconsistencies in your headings. Check, for instance, that you consistently use upper and lower case, and that the headings in each section are grammatically parallel.

Make sure that you use the editing commands needed to make the automatic table of contents work: In Word, for instance, use the Heading 1 through Heading 5 styles to set up the headings (control-alt-1 to control-alt-4 are usually configured as keyboard shortcuts for Headings 1 to 4) and when you insert the table of contents, ask for it to show up to 5 levels, and not just the default 3.

I. *Note Down All Your Ideas*

As you write, you'll often get interesting ideas that you can't act on immediately—for instance, because they relate to another section or to something that you should research.

Write down these ideas before you forget them. I prefer to record them in my main document—either in the computer or on the printout that I'm editing—tagged with some text, such as "**." You can put them into the section where they'll ultimately be discussed, in a master "to do" list at the top or bottom of the document, or even in whatever text you're currently writing. Because they're specially marked, you can easily find them later; and because they're written down, you won't lose what might be a great thought.

Likewise, at the end of a writing session, always write down what you plan to do next.[8] That way, you won't lose your train of thought, and will find it easier to start the next session.

J. *Things to Look For: Logic*

1. Categorical Assertions

Avoid "never" and "always," as in "this law would be completely unenforceable" or "could never be enforced." Completely? Never? Really? Modest claims may sometimes seem less rhetorically effective, but they're more likely to be right.

2. Insistence on Perfection

People often criticize laws by arguing that they're imperfect: "The law is targeted at preventing children from accidentally killing themselves or other children with a gun. However, the law itself would not adequately protect against all of the possible accidental handgun deaths."

This is a weak criticism. No law can prevent *all* instances of a certain kind of harm. The questions are usually whether the law does more harm than good, and whether other alternatives can do still better. You can't avoid these hard questions merely by showing that the law doesn't always do the good that it's meant to do. (This quote and most of the others in this chapter are drawn from real papers and articles that I've read.)

More broadly, be careful when you implicitly assume that the world is neatly divided into two categories—for instance, perfect laws and pointless laws. Such divisions often ignore the existence of a third category, such as laws that do something but not everything.

3. False Alternatives

"Is pornography free speech or hate speech?" "Are race-conscious affirmative action programs permissible or discriminatory?" "Should American foreign policy aim at making other countries fear us, or at getting them to work with us?"

The trouble with these either-or questions is that the answer may well be "both." Pornography might qualify as "hate speech" under some definition, but still be constitutionally protected. Race-conscious affirmative action programs might be discriminatory and yet constitutionally permissible. American foreign policy might aim at making some countries work with us by making them fear us.

Asking "X or Y?" tends to suggest that the answer must be one or the other. If this suggestion is incorrect, then asking the question will confuse the reader, and may make your argument unsound. And if you do think that X and Y should be mutually exclusive—that, for instance, hate speech should never be protected by the Free Speech Clause—you should demonstrate this mutual exclusiveness, rather than just assuming it by posing the "X or Y?" question.

4. Missing Pieces

A logical argument should consist of several steps that fit together, for instance: "All As are Bs. X is an A. Therefore, X is a B." Legal arguments aren't exercises in formal logic, but they must still fit logically, with no unproven connections.

Say your argument looks roughly like this:

(a) Classifications based on sex are subject to the most exacting scrutiny.

(b) Separate classes for boys and girls involve classifications based on sex.

(c) Therefore, separate classes for boys and girls are unconstitutional.

The pieces don't quite fit: Points (a) and (b) prove only that separate classes are subject to the most exacting scrutiny, not that they are unconstitutional. You must fill in the missing piece, by showing that the classification fails the exacting scrutiny.

Before writing your proof section, and again after finishing it, summarize each significant assertion in one sentence, much like the list I've just given. Then see if the assertions fit each other. If they don't fit together on your list, they probably don't fit together in the paper.

5.   Criticisms That Could Apply to Everything

It's not enough to say that a law "has a chilling effect," or "starts us down the slippery slope," or "imposes the majority's morality on the minority," or "intrudes on people's privacy." Most laws that constrain people's conduct—murder laws, antidiscrimination laws, bans on cruelty to animals—impose the majority's morality on the minority; sometimes that's good. Many laws have chilling effects or intrude on people's privacy; but we often tolerate this because these laws' good effects outweigh the bad. Almost every law potentially starts us down some slippery slope, but that's not reason enough to reject it.

Be specific. Explain why this chilling effect is worse than other chilling effects that we're willing to tolerate (and what exactly you mean by chilling effect). Explain why this slope is more slippery than others, or why it's wrong to impose this particular kind of moral principle on people, or why this intrusion on privacy is unjustified even though other intrusions are permissible.

Whenever you criticize a law, especially when you do it using generalities, *ask yourself whether the criticism could equally apply to laws that you endorse.* If it can, refine your criticism to make clear specifically why this law is bad when the others are good.

6.   Metaphors

Metaphors can make your writing more vivid, but they can also hide logical error and incompleteness.

Metaphors are literally false. Societies do not literally slip down slopes. Laws do not literally chill speech. These terms have some truth to them, but only to the extent that they describe *concrete mechanisms* and not just abstract metaphors. When we say "slippery slope," that's shorthand for "this seemingly unobjectionable decision may cause other, much more troublesome decisions in the future." When we say "this

77

speech restriction has a chilling effect,'' that's shorthand for ''this speech restriction may deter certain speech even though the restriction ostensibly doesn't cover that speech.''

Once you unpack the metaphor this way, you can see that you need to support it with a more concrete explanation. Why would this decision lead to other decisions in the future? What speech would be deterred by this restriction, and how?

Many people omit these explanations, perhaps because the metaphors sound self-explanatory. In the physical world, we can say ''Watch out for that driveway—the slope there is slippery'' without further explanation, because we know the mechanism that underlies the slippery slope: It's gravity coupled with inadequate friction.

But these physical mechanisms obviously don't carry over to slippery slopes in law; so when we use the term ''slippery slope'' metaphorically, *our argument is incomplete unless we give more details* about what the metaphor really means. Whenever you see a metaphor, ask yourself, ''To what actual phenomenon does this figurative usage refer?,'' and describe this phenomenon. If you think the metaphor helps people understand your point, you can still keep the metaphor as well as the actual description. But remember that the heart of your argument should be the real, not the figurative.

7.   Undefined Terms

Look skeptically at any abstraction that you mention but don't specifically define, such as ''paternalism,'' ''democratic legitimacy,'' ''fundamental fairness,'' ''evolving standards of decency,'' ''narrow tailoring,'' ''good faith,'' or the like. These abstractions can be useful, but they are vague enough that (1) the reader might not clearly understand what you mean by them, (2) you yourself might not clearly understand what you mean by them, and (3) you risk using them to mean different things in different cases.

Make clear what you mean by each term: What constitutes paternalism (whether good paternalism or bad)? How do you decide what's democratically legitimate and what isn't? Does fundamental fairness refer to an existing body of law, or just to your moral judgment? If it's the latter, what is that moral judgment, and why is it right? Are evolving standards of decency the standards of decency expressed in legislation throughout the states, or are they whatever standards the judges believe are decent? What is required to make a law narrowly tailored?

Many of these terms can't be defined precisely, and that may be fine. But if you find that they are too vague, you might ask yourself whether they really help your argument; and in any case, trying to give a clarifying definition can help you refine your argument, both for your own understanding and to make the argument easier for readers to follow.

8. Undefended Assertions, and "Arguably"/"Raises Concerns"

If you make an assertion, you need to be sure that it's adequately defended (unless it's obvious). Including "arguably" or "it can be argued that" isn't enough: It acknowledges that the statement is controversial, but it doesn't explain why the reader should accept your side of the controversy. If you think something is arguably true, then give the argument, and explain why it's better than the counterargument.

Likewise, it isn't enough to argue that some proposal "raises constitutional concerns" or "is troubling." If you think the proposal is actually unconstitutional, or actually unsound, explain why you think so.* It's not enough just to hint at the possibility, and to expect this hint to carry your argument.

* * *

All these points reinforce the need to go through many drafts, looking at your arguments with new eyes. The only way you can catch problems like these—or the writing errors mentioned below—is by repeatedly and carefully reading your own work.

K. *Things to Look For: Writing*

1. Paragraphs Lacking a Common Theme

Each paragraph should be about one main thought. The first sentence should usually express that thought; that's why it's often called the topic sentence. The other sentences should fit with that thought. If they don't, then they belong in a different paragraph.

---

* Showing the existence of "serious questions about the statute's constitutionality" may suffice when you're applying the rule that statutes should, if possible, be construed to avoid such questions. But even there it's not enough to say that the statute raises constitutional concerns—you have to show that they are indeed "serious" concerns.

2. Long Paragraphs

Avoid long paragraphs. People tend to digest one paragraph at a time, and if they see that they'll have to absorb twenty sentences, they may get intimidated and skip to the next paragraph.

Writers disagree to some extent about the best average paragraph length. I recommend two to four sentences; others like five or six. But I'm pretty sure that one-sentence paragraphs are usually too choppy, though they're sometimes good when introducing several longer paragraphs; and that once you get past six medium-length sentences or four longish ones, you'll be taxing many readers' attention spans.

A paragraph that's about one big thought can often be easily split into several paragraphs, each one about a smaller thought. Try to make sure that the split follows the natural structure of the discussion, and that each of the new paragraphs starts with a topic sentence.

Occasionally, you might want to split a paragraph where there's no natural paragraph break. If, for instance, you have a topic sentence followed by half a dozen sentence-long illustrations, you could split the paragraph just to give the reader a breather. Look over the result, though, and make sure that it doesn't seem too disconnected.

3. Inadequate Connections Between Paragraphs

Each paragraph should be logically linked to the one before it. When the reader starts reading a paragraph, he should understand its relationship to the preceding one.

This doesn't mean that you should start each paragraph with a transition like "Moreover" or "On the other hand." Transitions are sometimes helpful, but not always; and sometimes they're distracting. For instance, this paragraph is connected to the preceding one without an explicit transition—the pronoun "This" does the job.

Repeating a word or a concept from the previous paragraph, and especially from the paragraph's last sentence, is another connecting mechanism; so is the word "another." Feel free to change the part of speech when you repeat a word this way, for instance by using "connecting" in the first sentence of a paragraph to link back to "connected" in the last sentence of the previous one. Such links help you take the reader smoothly from thought to thought, making it clear how the thoughts fit.

4. Redundancy

When you see two sentences that express similar thoughts, try to eliminate one, or part of one. If you're intentionally restating a thought to make it clearer, try to make it clear the first time you say it. The phrase "in other words," in particular, is a clue that the first words you used aren't that good. Repetition annoys busy readers who want to get to the point quickly, and it can also confuse readers: If the second sentence makes the same point as the first sentence but uses slightly different words to do it, some readers will assume that the two sentences must say something different, and spend time looking for this nonexistent difference.

Likewise, watch out for phrases such as "any and all," "aid and abet," or "cease and desist," in which two words linked by an "and" or an "or" are, practically speaking, identical. Except when the redundant phrase has legal significance (for instance, "a cease-and-desist letter"), eliminate one of the components (making it "all," "aid," or "cease," or, better yet, "all," "help," or "stop").

These redundant couples are often clichés, but writers also often create their own, for instance "the new nouns generally tend to be more abstract and conceptual than the concrete actions and attributes that they replace" (a phrase from an earlier draft of this book). Perhaps "abstract" and "conceptual" might sometimes mean subtly different things, but not here. "Abstract" alone will do fine, and will keep the reader from wondering which nouns are more abstract and which ones are more conceptual.

Repetition is sometimes rhetorically useful for stressing an important point, and sometimes actually clarifies things. The introduction and the conclusion of an article, for instance, necessarily repeat some of what the body of the article says. Usually, though, redundancy makes your writing less effective.

5. Unnecessary Introductory Clauses

"*It should be mentioned that* knowledgeable gun owners already know that ...." "*In having researched the implications of the act,* I would recommend that ...." The italicized phrases add nothing: They're throat-clearing—things people say before they start getting to the point. Delete them.

81

6. Other Unnecessary Phrases

More broadly, each sentence and each clause should make some specific point that's useful to your argument. Consider one example from a student paper: "The state legislature should reject this proposal because it is the wrong solution." What extra information does "because it is the wrong solution" convey to the reader?

Likewise, consider another example:

> Given the large number of accidental firearms injuries among young people that occur annually in this country, everyone would agree that firearms safety is a matter of great public concern.

On that level of generality, everyone does agree—to the point that the sentence adds nothing substantively, and is such an obvious platitude that it adds nothing rhetorically either.

Either delete the sentence or make it more concrete. For example, it turns out that in 2000, about 85 children age fourteen or under died in firearms accidents in the U.S., and about 1850 were nonfatally injured in such accidents (about 1100 were treated and released, while about 750 were transferred or hospitalized).[9] If you replace the vague phrase "large number" with the specific number, you'll be saying something that might be news to many readers, and you'll be giving readers a better idea of just how concerned they should be about this.

Finally, consider these opening paragraphs of a draft article on campaign finance law (also mentioned at p. 33 above):

> Campaign speech has long been a controversial topic among scholars and commentators. Much attention has been devoted to the Supreme Court's treatment of individual expenditures, contributions and spending in *Buckley v. Valeo*. Congress' recent consideration of campaign finance reform provides an ideal opportunity to revisit the 1976 Supreme Court decision that addressed the free speech implications of limits on federal campaign-related activities.

> This essay briefly discusses the effects of such limits on individual speech, the disproportionate treatment of speech by the media and justifications presented by several members of the Court in the 2000 decision, *Nixon v. Shrink Missouri Government PAC*.

> Let me begin by giving a concrete situation. Imagine you are outraged about a particular candidate's stand on something. [More concrete details follow, aimed at showing that there's a basic First Amendment right to spend money to express your views about candidates.] . . .

What does the first sentence add? Very little: Virtually all readers will already know how controversial the subject is. The same goes for the second sentence. The third sentence says something nontrivial, by suggesting that this article is relevant to "Congress' recent consideration of campaign finance reform," but most of the rest of the sentence isn't helpful either.

That's a lot of unnecessary generalities—and at the very beginning of the article, which sets the tone for what follows. Here's an alternative, with the surplusage cut out:

> Imagine you are outraged about a particular candidate's stand on something. [More concrete details] . . .
>
> May the law restrict this sort of speech, in the name of preventing corruption or equalizing people's voices? May the law allow the media to editorialize about elections while limiting speech by others? These questions are made especially relevant by the enactment of the new campaign finance bill. This essay will briefly discuss them, with a special focus on the Justices' arguments in *Nixon v. Shrink Missouri Government PAC.*

Not perfect—the last two sentences are clunkier than they should be—but at least each part adds something to the argument.

7. Legalese/Bureaucratese

Write like normal people speak, not like lawyers or bureaucrats tend to write. Don't write "Opposition to the bill is needed on the grounds that the means will produce little or no desirable ends." Saying "We should oppose the bill because it won't work" "Legislators should oppose the bill because [fill in the specific reason]," or even just "The proposal won't work" would make the same point in plain English.

Likewise, replace "Guns have a far greater utilitarian value than . . ." with "Guns are far more useful than . . . ." Instead of "could negatively affect the accessibility of handguns," write "could make handguns less accessible."

a. These three examples all illustrate one common cause of legalese: "nominalization"—turning verbs, adjectives, and adverbs into nouns or noun phrases. The verb-heavy phrase "we *should oppose*" becomes the noun-focused "*opposition* to the bill is needed." The adverb phrase "are *far more useful than*" becomes the noun-focused "have a *far greater utilitarian value* than." The adjective phrase "could make handguns *less accessible*" becomes the noun-focused "could negatively affect *the accessibility* of handguns."

Nominalization tends to add words, which makes text longer, and to add prepositional or verb phrases, which makes text more complex. It also tends to make the writing less concrete and thus less lively, because the new nouns ("opposition," "value," and "accessibility") generally tend to be more abstract than the concrete actions ("should oppose") and attributes ("more useful" or "less accessible") that they replace. If you see an abstract noun, ask whether you can replace it with the concrete verb, adjective, or adverb that the noun phrase embodies.

b. Legal writers also tend to use long phrases instead of their short synonyms. Instead of "many," lawyers often write "a large number of." "Near" becomes "in close proximity to." "The legislature" turns into "the legislative branch of government."

Sometimes the long phrases might seem to add some important nuance—for instance, a person may write "the legislative branch of government" to highlight the distinction between the legislature and other branches of government. But even then, simpler versions can often express the nuance equally well; referring to "the executive," "the legislature," and "the judiciary" probably highlights the distinction between the branches equally well. If you see a formal-sounding phrase that seems to represent just one basic concept, ask whether one word could do the job instead.

c. Some argue that formal words and legal clichés add dignity to prose. And some prose does sound better when it's more formal—"Four score and seven years ago" sounds better in the Gettysburg Address than "Eighty-seven years ago" or "In 1776."

But the Gettysburg Address was an oration in honor of fallen soldiers; Lincoln had a captive audience that was disposed to agree with him; and the entire address was only three minutes long.[10] Most law review articles won't satisfy any of these criteria. For practical reasons, they should be clear and easy to read; and while you'd like them to seem intellectually hefty and sometimes even emotionally stirring, formal language isn't likely to give you that.

So as you read your draft, ask yourself for each sentence: Do ordinary people talk this way? Would I ever hear this from an articulate nonlawyer friend over dinner? "Opposition to the bill is needed on the grounds that the means will produce little or no desirable ends" flunks this test.

If you really learn this rule, you'll be set. But in the meantime, Appendix I (p. 165) gives some tips on particular words and phrases you might want to avoid; and if you go to *http://volokh.com/writing*, you can download a macro that will automatically identify for you most of the words and phrases listed in the Appendix.

8. Unnecessary Abstractions

You should make your argument using words that clearly describe the real problems that people face, rather than talking about the problems in abstract terms (even if the abstract terms aren't especially legalese). Consider the following phrases:

> . . . when law enforcement is unavailable.

> Considering the amount of violence that is connected with guns . . .

> . . . will have a positive effect.

They are written in fairly plain English, and aren't hard to understand— but they make their points through abstract terms such as "unavailable," "violence," and "positive effect," and the circumlocution "law enforcement."

When you want someone to protect you, whom do you want? Your visceral, real-life answer will be "the police," not "law enforcement." What do you want them to do? Your normal answer will be "come in time," not "be available." "When the police can't come in time" quickly engages the reader's practical concerns; "when law enforcement is unavailable" doesn't. (I assume that the "[come in time] to prevent a killing, rape, or robbery" is implicit from context; if it isn't, then some such phrase should be included.)

Likewise, instead of "Considering the amount of violence that is connected with guns," try "Considering how many people are killed, injured, or threatened with guns." Killings, injuries, and threats are what people *really* worry about; "violence" is just the abstract term for that. Readers will intellectually understand what "violence" means, but they won't be as engaged by it as they would be by "killed, injured, or threatened."

Instead of "will have a positive effect," describe the actual effect, for instance "will prevent many murders and suicides." No one wants "positive effects" in the abstract; they want specific, concrete benefits, and if you explain the benefits, people will be more persuaded.

One more example:

> The waiting period provides a vital time frame, which allows an individual the time to reconsider their actions and consequently, lives will be saved.

This sentence contains several writing glitches; "individual" is legalese for "person," "a vital time frame" is vague, and "their" is plural while "individual" is singular. But the deeper problem is that the sentence is written using unnecessary abstractions. A better formulation would be:

> The waiting period can prevent impulsive murders and suicides, by giving people time to calm down [*optional:* and reconsider their plans].

Instead of the general "time to reconsider their actions" and "lives will be saved," this explains concretely which actions (impulsive murders and suicides) will be reconsidered and which lives will be saved. It provides more substantive details, describes a concrete scenario for the reader (an impulsive person needs to calm down, or else he'll commit murder or suicide), and thus makes the argument more persuasive.

There are two exceptions to this preference for the concrete. First, sometimes you need to use a term that's more abstract but more precise. For instance, "murder" is usually a better, more concrete term than "homicide," but if you are talking about a study that measures all homicides (including manslaughter, justifiable homicide, and excusable homicide), you need to use the more accurate term.

Second, sometimes you intentionally want to soften the emotional force of a claim, either because you fear that the issue may be too viscerally engaging (part of the reason that some articles use "sexual assault" instead of "rape"), or because you're describing the other side's argument. This second reason is not entirely praiseworthy, but it may be tolerable; you have an obligation to describe the counterarguments honestly, thoroughly, and clearly, but you need not frame them in the most emotionally forceful way possible.

But these are exceptions. The rule is to talk about what actually matters to the reader (the police not coming in time) and not about abstractions (law enforcement being unavailable).

9. Passive Voice

Many people recommend that you turn the passive voice—"The action was done by this person" (the object was verbed by the subject) or just "The action was done"—into the active voice, "This person did this action" (the subject verbed the object).

This is generally good advice. Passive voice often makes writing less direct: "Passive voice should be avoided by you" is worse than "Avoid the passive voice." It also sometimes conceals responsibility, as in the famous "Mistakes were made" used as a substitute for "We made mistakes."

But if your discussion focuses more on the object than on the subject (the actor), you might want to use the passive voice, which has a similar focus. If you're writing about the USA Patriot Act, for instance, the passive sentence "The Act was adopted shortly after the September 11 attacks" may be better than the active "Congress adopted the Act shortly after the September 11 attacks." The passive voice properly focuses the discussion on the Act, rather than on Congress.

10. Clichés

Generally avoid overused phrases, such as (to borrow examples that I've cut from drafts of this book) "more than meets the eye," "law of the land," "flat wrong," "time and time again," "mix and match," "done to death," "abandon ship," "chock full," or "go back to square one."

These phrases may seem like colorful intensifiers that catch the reader's attention; and sometimes they indeed do that, which is why the advice "avoid clichés" sometimes seems overstated. But the advice is usually sound. These phrases once (I almost wrote "once upon a time") were novel and vivid, and added flair to people's writing. But overuse has drained most clichés of this capacity. And because authors tend to overestimate their own wittiness, they often think that a cliché will add color even when it really doesn't.

There's thus little advantage to using clichés, and there are disadvantages. Some clichés annoy some readers; and almost all clichés make sentences longer and more complex. Each one may not make much difference, but the extra mental translation that they require can add up. And clichés keep you from inventing your own original imagery, which would be helpful precisely because it's fresh to the reader.

11. Figurative Phrases

Most clichés and all metaphors (see p. 77) are figurative phrases: They use words and phrases that mean something other than their literal meaning (for instance, "like a bull in a china shop"). Figurative phrasing is sometimes helpful, but it's often dangerous precisely because it uses terms in their nonliteral sense. You should use figurative terms sparingly, and you should always be aware of the literal meaning as well as the figurative when you do use them.

a. The first danger of the figurative was mentioned in the discussion of metaphors: Writers sometimes *assume that the figurative usage will do the work of persuading people or explaining the proposal*. But "allow-

87

ing courts to decide this would be like putting a bull in a china shop" is not a complete argument; "courts should balance the freedom of speech and the need for individual privacy" is not a complete proposal. They become complete only when the writer answers the underlying questions: Exactly why are courts incompetent at deciding this? Exactly how should courts deal with speech that reveals private information about others?

If you had used literal language, e.g., "courts aren't going to do a good job of deciding questions like this," you'd have seen the need to flesh out the argument. But figurative language, by hiding the literal meaning, can also hide this need.

b. The second danger is *forgetting that the figurative phrase has two different meanings*, and using the figurative meaning without realizing that the literal meaning will distract or confuse the reader.

i. *Mixed metaphors*, such as "the political equation was thus saturated with kerosene," are one example of this.[11] Standing alone, "the political equation" and "saturated with kerosene" would just convey their figurative meanings, and their literal meanings would be largely ignored. But when you put them together, readers will notice their incompatible literal meanings, and be distracted (and unintentionally amused). My favorite, possibly apocryphal, example: "This field of research is so virginal that no human eye has ever set foot in it."[12]

ii. Even a single figurative usage can have its literal meaning *unintentionally highlighted by surrounding concepts*: "The felony murder rule has been done to death in the literature" is either a weak (and macabre) intentional joke or a weak unintentional one. "Done to death" on its own just conveys its figurative meaning of "exhaustively covered," but when it's used while discussing felony murder, readers will think of the literal meaning as well, and be distracted. The distraction might be justified if you think the joke is funny enough, but usually it isn't.

iii. Figurative usages that allude to some literary work or historical practice may *clash with their original meaning*. To "decimate," for instance, originally meant to kill every tenth person as a collective punishment (hence the joke that "You can tell the ancient Romans were tough—in their language, 'to kill every tenth person as a collective punishment' was one word"). The figurative meaning, which is "to dramatically reduce," is now well established, but some people are still reminded of the old usage, which can either distract or annoy them.

Likewise, "East is East and West is West, and never the twain shall meet" is sometimes used to suggest that two cultures are irreconcilable. But Kipling's poem continues with "but there is neither East nor West, nor border, breed, nor birth, When two strong men stand face to face, tho' they come from the ends of the earth"—and people who are familiar with the poem will thus be reminded of the exact opposite of what the person who is quoting the "East is East" phrase is asserting.

You might think that such objections are pedantic; after all, you're using the modern meaning, not the original one. But when a writer chooses to express the modern meaning using a literary or historical allusion, he brings the literary or historical origin to the minds of those readers who know the origin. And if that original meaning distracts the reader from the actual meaning that the writer wanted to evoke, that's the writer's fault.

c. Figurative usages are *often misused*, because people don't think about (or don't understand) the literal meaning. "Back to ground zero," for instance, is often used instead of "back to square one." "Ground zero" is the location where a bomb is detonated, not the first step of a long task. But the similarity of "ground zero" and "square one," coupled with writers' lack of attention to the terms' literal meanings, makes it easy to confuse the two.

Likewise, "free rein," "toe the line," and "tough row to hoe" are often miswritten as "free reign," "tow the line," and "tough road to hoe." Even writers who would rarely misspell a literally used word may fall into these traps for figurative phrases, because the phrases' literal origins—which provide an important clue about their spelling—are often forgotten.

d. Writers are often *tempted into using figurative phrases* even when the phrase isn't quite right for the occasion. Thus, "raises the question" often becomes "begs the question"; "begs the question" traditionally refers to the fallacy of assuming the very point that you're trying to prove, but because the phrase seems so colorful, many people use it in a broader, and incorrect, sense. Likewise, a person's changing his behavior, even incrementally, becomes "the leopard changing its spots," even though the latter phrase generally refers not to all changes but specifically to radical ones.

So if you think some figurative phrase can make a point more vivid, use it, but only after considering both (1) whether the phrase really adds something, and (2) whether the literal meaning of the phrase might weaken your point more than the figurative enhances it. And always second-guess yourself whenever you use a figurative term unintentionally; many such uses prove to be unhelpful.

Finally, never, ever use the word "literally" when you mean "figuratively," as in "[T]he number of lawyers in the United States has literally exploded over the last 53 years." *Literally* exploded?

12. Unduly Harsh Criticism

Be understated in your criticisms, even if they're well founded. Don't call your opponents' arguments "fraudulent," "nonsense," "ridiculous," "silly," or even "egregiously wrong." Use "mistaken," "unsound," "erroneous," or other mild criticisms instead. People will get your message, and will be more disposed to accept it precisely because it's understated.

Why?

(a) Overstating your argument *raises your burden of proof.* Call an argument "fraudulent," and skeptical readers might say "Wait, is it really fraudulent, or could it just be an honest error?"; and this will distract them from your more important claim, which is that the argument is just wrong. Likewise, call the argument "irrational," and skeptical readers may try to find some reasonableness in it. You don't want to weaken your claims by making unproven and unnecessary allegations.

(b) *No one likes a bully.* Excessive harshness may alienate readers and make them sympathize with your adversaries.

(c) *Invective often hides lack of substance.* Readers realize this, and become suspicious when they hear overheated rhetoric.

(d) *Readers are less likely to tolerate harsh criticism by juniors—* such as law students or young lawyers—than similar criticism by respected scholars. By all means, pick fights with the Big Guns; your professor and other readers will admire your pluck. But be scrupulously polite to the people you criticize: A polite upstart is more tolerated than a rude one.

(e) There's *no need to make unnecessary enemies.* When you're applying for a job, and Justice X's former law clerk is reading your article, you'll be glad that you called Justice X's arguments "mistaken" rather than "stupid." This shouldn't stop you from expressing disagreement; people respect honest disagreement. But they don't respect rudeness, or even borderline rudeness, especially rudeness to people they know and like.

13. Personalized Criticism

Attack arguments, not people. Most readers will react better to "this argument is wrong because . . ." than to "Volokh is wrong because . . . ." Likewise, when you're criticizing an argument, don't call it Volokh's argument. Label it by name ("the cost-lowering slippery slope argument") or just say "the argument," if it's clear from context which argument you're referring to. Of course, properly attribute your adversary's argument, but do it in the footnotes, or with no more than one named reference in the text.

This sort of circumlocution helps readers feel that your disagreements are substantive, not personal. There's nothing inherently *rude* about criticizing a person's argument using his name, but such criticism tends to come across as unduly combative, even when it's not intended that way. And the more substantively devastating your criticism is, the more you should keep the devastated author's name out of it.

14. Acronyms

Acronyms (such as SSA, FIFO, DBA, TLA, and so on) tend to make a work less accessible, at least for readers who aren't already thoroughly familiar with them. This is especially so if a reader sees several such acronyms on the same page.

Some acronyms are unavoidable, and are so standard that most readers won't really notice them; everyone knows about the EPA and the FCC, and most people who read about religious freedom law know about RFRA (the Religious Freedom Restoration Act). Calling these entities by something other than their acronyms will be jarring and unnecessarily wordy.

But don't create your own acronyms, and try to avoid using preexisting acronyms that are relatively unfamiliar to most readers. For instance, if you're writing about the Gun Free School Zones Act, don't call it GFSZA—call it "the Act," since it's probably the only Act you'll be discussing in detail. If you're talking about slippery slope arguments, don't call them SSAs; spell out the phrase, or just say "such arguments" if your meaning is clear from context. Shorter is usually better, but not when you get brevity by making the article seem forbidding to casual readers.

15. Word Choice Errors

a. *Simple error.* "The police already have alternate counts to chase criminals"—not quite right. "Citizens' suspicions of intrusive gun control laws are at a height"; one can see what the author is getting at, but "at a height" is not the best phrase here.

b. *Inattentiveness to usage.* A more subtle problem is inattentiveness to the way words are normally used. Consider the phrase "the crime is not that serious (it is only negligent)." There's no inherent reason that we can't say "negligent crimes"; after all, we say "negligent homicide" or "negligent misrepresentation." But people don't in fact use this phrase.

Likewise, the phrase "crimes done in the heat of passion" is not logically wrong, but it is unidiomatic—crimes are generally "committed" rather than "done," and readers may find "crimes done" to be odd and jarring. Ask yourself, as you do when looking for legalese: "Do people actually talk this way?"

c. *Inattentiveness to literal meaning.* Consider the sentence "Firearms are one of the most lethal forms of suicide." It's clear what this means, but if you look closely, it's not literally accurate, for two reasons. First, all *suicide* (as opposed to attempts to commit suicide) is by definition completely lethal. Second, firearms are a *means* to commit suicide, not a form of suicide. "Firearms are one of the most lethal means for committing suicide" would be better, though "Suicide attempts with guns are especially likely to succeed" might be more accurate still.

This sort of objection may be pedantic, but many readers will make it. Consciously or not, some people may see such logical errors as evidence of an illogical mind; and sometimes (though not in this example), the errors will make the sentence ambiguous or hard to understand. True, English is full of illogical idioms (for instance, "ice cream" isn't made of ice—"iced cream" would have been more logical), but outside these well-established idioms, you're better off using words as logically as possible.

d. *Errors obscured by intervening words.* Word choice errors are particularly likely if the two parts of the unidiomatic or illogical phrase are separated by other words. In "crimes done in the heat of passion," the unidiomatic usage ("crimes done") is pretty clear; but in "crimes which would have been done in the heat of passion," it's less obvious. There's no solution for this except careful proofreading.

L. Proofreading

Words are the lawyer's most important tools. If you use the wrong word, or make a minor grammar, spelling, or punctuation error, you come across as a craftsman who doesn't know how to use his tools. You lose credibility, even if the substance of what you're saying is sound.

Thus, as you read your article in each editing pass, ask yourself the following questions:

1. (For each sentence:) What information does this sentence communicate to readers that they *don't already know*?

2. (For each sentence:) Has this information—or even part of it— *already been communicated by a previous sentence*?

3. (For each sentence:) Are this sentence and the previous sentence *so closely related* that part of the first sentence is repeated in this one?

4. (For each word, phrase, or sentence:) Can I *eliminate this without changing the meaning*?*

5. (For each phrase in a sentence:) Is this how *normal people talk*?

6. (For each word:) Does this word communicate *exactly what I want it to*?

7. (For each noun:) *Should this noun be a verb, adjective, or adverb* instead?

For more tips, check out Bruce Ross–Larson's *Edit Yourself,* which focuses mostly on word and sentence edits; C. Edward Good's *Mightier than the Sword* and *A Grammar Book for You and I;* Bryan Garner's *Elements of Legal Style;* and Strunk & White's *The Elements of Style,* the classic general writing guide.

M. Editing: Two Exercises

Practice these suggestions using two concrete examples. Both are paragraphs from real seminar papers written in response to the following assignment:

Your boss, Senator Elaine Mandel, is a member of the State Senate Committee on the Judiciary. The Committee will shortly consider the

---

* The careful reader may have noticed that these questions, aimed largely at finding redundancy, are themselves redundant. This is intentional: When you are looking for things that are often overlooked—such as redundancies or other writing problems—it's often useful to look for them using several slightly different approaches. This, though, is one of the rare situations where redundancy is helpful.

proposed Child Firearms Safety Act, which states that "Any person who lives in the same household as a minor and who possesses a handgun shall store the handgun unloaded and in a locked container." Please write a short memo advising the Senator whether she should vote for the law.

Here are the opening paragraphs from the two papers:

The Child Firearm Safety Act as currently written is a well intentioned piece of legislation which will likely have little effect on the incidence of minors accidentally killed by handguns. However, with some critical modifications the act could play a significant role in lowering the number of minors lost to handgun accidents each year. These modifications should include: compelling either that the gun be kept in a locked container *or* unloaded; the inclusion of long guns in the Act; and making violation of the Act a felony offense.

and

The proposed Child Firearms Safety Act (the "bill") is an inconsequential piece of legislation. Aside from the significant political impact of the bill, it carries little weight and makes little difference. Despite public misconceptions, the few benefits of the bill, notably the probable slight decrease in the number of childhood gun accidents, do not exceed the drawbacks, such as the inaccessibility of guns during a home invasion and loss of civil liberties. Therefore, unless some strong amendments are made to the bill, I recommend that you oppose the bill.

Try rewriting each to make it clearer and about 50% shorter; I give some possible answers in Appendix II.A, p. 171.

V. USING EVIDENCE CORRECTLY

> "Like the thirteenth chime of a clock, which is
> not only wrong by itself, but casts doubt on all
> that came before it."
>
> —Proverb

In trying to prove your claim, you'll use a lot of evidence—cases, statutes, historical facts, social science data, and so on. You need to use this evidence correctly.

Part of the reason is honesty and professional responsibility, but another part is self-interest: Instructors don't like errors, and neither do other readers. A couple of mistakes, even on tangential matters, can undermine the credibility of all the sound arguments you make.

If some evidence seemingly contradicts your claim, you can confront the problem and explain why your claim is nonetheless sound. But if you try to hide the problem by misdescribing the evidence, you'll damage your argument much more than if you had been candid about the issue. This Part offers suggestions for avoiding common errors in the use of evidence, together with some examples drawn from real cases and articles (though with the authors' names intentionally omitted).

The examples are ones that I've run across in my own research, so you'll find them skewed towards those areas in which I work. But you can find similar problems in any field of scholarship, coming from all perspectives, left, center, right, and beyond, and even in the work of otherwise careful writers.

A. Read, Quote and Cite the Original Source

Whenever you make a claim about some source, you nearly always must read the original source. Do *not* rely on an intermediate source—whether a law review article or a case—that cites the original.

1. Legal Evidence

If you're discussing a case or a statute, read, quote, and cite the case or statute itself. Do not rely on other cases, articles, treatises, or encyclopedias that mention the source.* Check the original. If you can't

---

* One exception: Old sources are sometimes reprinted in authoritative compendia; because the purpose of these works is to be authoritative sources, they tend to be quite

find the original, ask your librarians; they will usually be glad to help you.

Intermediate sources may seem authoritative, but they're often unreliable, whether because of bias or honest mistake. You can't let their mistakes become your mistakes.

Here's an example, from an interdisciplinary faculty-edited journal published by a leading university press:

> On the one occasion when such [gun control] legislation was over-turned, in *Bliss v. Commonwealth* (1822), the Kentucky Supreme Court ruled that state regulation of firearms violated the state's militia amendment, which granted an explicitly individual right to bear arms (12 Ky. 90). In response, the legislature immediately amended the state constitution to allow such legislation, rewriting the militia amendment to more closely match the federal Constitution's Second Amendment (Kentucky 1835).[13]

Seems reliable, no? Well, it turns out that:

(a) *Bliss* did not involve "the state's militia amendment," but rather a constitutional provision that never mentioned the militia: "That the rights of the citizens to bear arms in defence of themselves and the State shall not be questioned."[14] The militia provisions were in a separate article of the constitution.[15] And the provision was technically not an amendment, since it was enacted together with the rest of the state constitution.

(b) The legislature did not immediately amend the state constitution. The constitution provided no mechanisms for amendment,[16] and the provision was changed only when a new constitution was adopted in 1850—28 years after *Bliss*.[17] The Kentucky 1835 source, which actually gives an 1834 publication date on its title page, does not show any change to the original provision.

(c) The 1850 revision did not make the right to bear arms provision "more closely match the federal Constitution's Second Amendment"—it added the clause "but the general assembly may pass laws to prevent persons from carrying concealed arms," which doesn't appear in the Second Amendment.

well-checked and reliable. If your librarian tells you that some such source has a good reputation, you can generally count on it. FRANCIS N. THORPE, THE FEDERAL AND STATE CONSTITUTIONS (1909), for instance, is a reliable reference for pre–1909 state constitutions.

Whoops! Pretty embarrassing for the author. But if you cited this as evidence of what *Bliss* said and what the Kentucky legislature did, then it would be embarrassing for *you*.

There are many other examples, some of which themselves arise from scholars not checking the original source, and thus repeating the intermediate source's error. For instance, several articles claim that the common phrase "rule of thumb" originated in a "common law rule that a husband could beat his wife without legal sanction if he used a rod no thicker than his thumb." This etymological claim—like many interesting etymological claims—appears to be mythical.[18] But it has appeared in many reputable journals, and is poised to lead still more people into error.

Even Supreme Court opinions can contain mistakes; for instance, *Reno v. ACLU*, where the Court struck down the first Internet indecency ban (the CDA), said the following to distinguish two earlier cases:

> The breadth of the CDA's coverage is wholly unprecedented. Unlike the regulations upheld in *Ginsberg* [*v. New York*, 390 U.S. 629 (1968),] and [*FCC v.*] *Pacifica* [*Foundation*, 438 U.S. 726 (1978)], the scope of the CDA is not limited to commercial speech or commercial entities.[19]

Sounds like you can confidently assert, citing *Reno*, that the restrictions in *Ginsberg* and *Pacifica* were limited to commercial speech or commercial entities.

Unfortunately, the *Reno* opinion was wrong. The *Ginsberg* law, which barred the sales of certain sexually themed magazines to minors, was not limited to commercial speech: Such magazines, even ones sold for money, do not qualify as commercial speech, a term that generally refers only to commercial advertising.[20] The *Pacifica* regulation was not limited either to commercial speech or to commercial entities; the broadcast in *Pacifica* itself was noncommercial speech carried by a nonprofit, noncommercial radio station.[21] Whoops.

If you want to cite *Reno* as evidence of how the *Reno* Court *treated* the precedents, that's fine, though from the context it doesn't look like the Court was intentionally trying to redefine the terms "commercial speech" and "commercial entities." But you shouldn't cite *Reno* as evidence of what actually happened in *Ginsberg* and *Pacifica*—read, quote, and cite the precedents directly.

One significant exception: Judges' discussions of the factual findings in the litigation itself tend to be fairly reliable. These discussions aren't perfect, but they're generally good enough for you to trust. Even in this context, though, consult the most thorough available version of the factual findings—if the trial court's finding of facts are available, read them, rather than just relying on the appellate court's account.

2. Historical, Economic, or Scientific Evidence

If you're making a claim about:

* history (the Framing generation thought this-and-such),
* economics (demand for these sorts of goods operates this way),
* social or physical science (people in this experiment behaved this way),
* or any other specialized discipline,

you should read, quote, and cite a work in that discipline. Do not rely on law review articles that make this assertion.

People who write law review articles are usually not experts in history, economics, and science. Some are quite knowledgeable in those fields, but some have learned just enough to be dangerous.

If possible, you should go to the ultimate source, such as a historical document or a scientific study. Many of the ultimate sources are available in your university library—your law school reference librarians can help you find them, and possibly even borrow them for you from another library, if necessary. Law students often overestimate the difficulty of getting books from other libraries. Law school librarians tend to be quite ready to help students (or recent alumni) with this sort of research.

Sometimes, you might have to rely on an intermediate source. The ultimate source might be too technical for you to adequately understand. The authors of a book may be expressing their own expert judgment based on a wide range of materials, and no single ultimate source will directly support that judgment. Or you might just not have the time to go through a large body of original material.

Still, you should rely on such secondary sources as rarely as possible, because each time you rely on them, you risk inadvertently incorporating their errors or at least their selective quotations. And you particularly should not rely on secondary sources *outside the underlying discipline*, such as law review articles that cite history books; there, the risk of error is too high.

There's one important exception to this: In some fields, such as legal history or law and economics, the original scholarship is itself published in legal journals. So if you're making a claim about, for instance, the Framers' understanding of the Fourth Amendment (a historical question), citing a law review article may make sense, so long as the cited article is the original historical work, and so long as you read all the historical sources that you plan on citing.

But if you're making a claim about the demographics of the various states shortly after independence, don't cite a law review article for that proposition. Find the books that the article cites (or, better yet, the sources on which the history books rely), and read, quote, and cite them.

3. Newspapers

Newspaper articles often omit critical details, or err in the details they do include. This makes it risky to rely on them.

Most reporters are generalists, who write about subjects on which they aren't expert. They also tend to write under tight deadlines, and with strict word limits. Their work is then edited by editors who often know still less about the subject, and have even less time.

Reporters also rarely check the original sources; instead, they usually rely on some supposed expert's judgment. Moreover, in my experience, reporters rarely check back with the experts to make sure their quotes were accurately transcribed and edited. (One story, for instance, rendered my reference to a "marina operator's right to his property" as a "marina operator's right to hypocrisy."[22])

This unreliability may not be the reporters' fault; they might be doing the best they can, given their deadlines. But the result is that their work is much less reliable than even the imperfectly reliable law review articles, which at least are written by people who are relatively expert, who have time to check their sources, and who know that they must include footnotes that someone will check. Think back on how many errors or important omissions you've seen in newspaper articles about subjects you know, and you'll get a sense of how often newspaper accounts err about all things.

So here are some guidelines:

(a) Never rely on a newspaper article's account of *a published case, a statute, or other legal source*. The articles are too often wrong, and it's easy enough for you to check the source yourself.

(b) Don't rely on newspaper descriptions of *legal documents* (such as complaints, briefs, or unpublished court decisions), *or historical or scientific studies* if the information is at all important to your claim; get the underlying legal document or historical or scientific source. You can often get copies of unpublished decisions, complaints, pleadings, and other items from the lawyers involved in the case. Your research librarians might also help you track down these sources.

(c) If the newspaper *doesn't cite the original source*, do a LEXIS NEWS;CURNWS,ARCNWS or WESTLAW ALLNEWSPLUS search for stories that mention the same assertion. Some of the other stories may give more details that can help you track down the original document. (For instance, if you did this for the famous claim that Vice President Dan Quayle once told Latin Americans that "I wish I'd studied Latin at school so I could talk to you in your own language," you'd find that the story was made up as a joke, and then repeated as if it were true.[23])

(d) *Sometimes the newspaper is the original source*, for instance when it repeats what someone told the reporter, or said at some event; you might then have to use the newspaper account. Keep in mind, though, the risk that the newspaper may have erred or quoted someone out of context. For instance, in early 2003, several op-eds ridiculed former Representative Cynthia McKinney for saying that "In no other country on the planet do so many people have so little as they do in this country"—a patently false claim. Listening to the CSPAN video of the speech, however, reveals that McKinney actually said "In no other *rich democracy* on this planet do so many people have so little" (emphasis added), a *very* different and more plausible assertion.[24]

Therefore, if you can, e-mail the quoted speaker to verify the quote. You can often find e-mail addresses through search engines, especially when you're looking for the address of an academic or a lawyer. You can also find many lawyers' phone numbers and e-mail addresses through the WESTLAW WLD directory, the LEXIS MARHUB library, or the Web sites of state bars. And if the quote was from a publicly broadcast speech, check whether a video of the program might exist online.

(e) *If your only source for a proposition is a newspaper article*, or some person quoted (or misquoted) in the article, acknowledge in the text the possibility that this is not a highly reliable source (e.g., by using a phrase such as "press accounts report that"). And if there is reason to doubt the quoted source's accuracy, for instance if the source is an interested party, or is talking about something that he might have misperceived or misunderstood, you should note that explicitly.

100

(f) In any event, if you are citing a newspaper article for a proposition, *make clear*—either in the footnote, or, if this is important, in the text—

    i. the nature of the article (is it an opinion piece or supposedly objective reporting?),

    ii. the nature of the source (whom does the article quote for the proposition, and what are the source's possible biases?), and

    iii. any other reasons why the source might be inaccurate.

On the last point, here's an example. According to one history book,

> Supreme Court Justice Antonin Scalia agreed with this view that citizens have a constitutionally protected right to own machine guns.

Seems like a reliable claim, written by a history professor. We're all set to say "Justice Scalia takes the view that citizens have a constitutional right to own machine guns," citing the book.

But have a look at the source on which the book relies, the *Baltimore Sun*, April 30, 1999, at 27A. (The citation in the endnote contains only this, with no further information.) Here's how the article—which turns out to be an opinion column entitled *Scalia Is Wrong on Guns*—begins; all the relevant material is in these paragraphs:

> Five days before two teen-agers went on a murderous shooting rampage in a Colorado high school, U.S. Supreme Court Justice Antonin Scalia told a group of students at the Park School in Baltimore County that if he had his way, people would have more—not less—access to deadly weapons.

> At a small luncheon following his speech to 300 students there, Justice Scalia said that citizens have a right to own machine guns, said . . . a 17–year-old Park senior.

> Pressing the outer limits of his thinking on this matter, [the student]—who has earned early admission to Princeton University—said she asked Justice Scalia if he thought people should also "be allowed to have hand-held rockets that can bring down airplanes."

> After a moment of contemplation, Justice Scalia told [the student] he didn't like that idea. Justice Scalia fancies himself an "originalist"—someone who thinks the Constitution means today exactly what it meant when it was adopted two centuries ago.

> So not surprisingly, Justice Scalia says the language of the Second Amendment, which gives citizens the right to bear arms, is a license for people to amass a nearly limitless arsenal of weapons.

The book, then, was indirectly relying on a high school student's paraphrase of what she recalled Justice Scalia saying at a private lunch.

It's certainly possible that the student was right. It's also possible, though, that she may have misheard, misremembered, or misinterpreted Scalia's position (for instance, treating a devil's advocate argument as a sincere assertion), or omitted some explicit or implied qualifier. It's likewise possible that the student was correct, but the opinion writer who quoted the student misinterpreted or misdescribed the student's account. We can't tell for sure—but the book's author should have alerted us to these uncertainties, by providing more than an unqualified assertion that "Justice Antonin Scalia agreed with this view that citizens have a constitutionally protected right to own machine guns," with no explanation of the possible problems with the source.

So if you want to say something about Scalia's views in your own article, you certainly shouldn't just cite the book or the newspaper column. The source here seems so potentially unreliable that you might not want to use it at all. But if you do use it, you should at least make clear to the readers the possible accuracy problems—chiefly that the statement was made to a small audience, that there's only one source, and that the source's statement is itself being reported second-hand. For instance, you might say

> Supreme Court Justice Antonin Scalia said at a private talk that citizens have a constitutionally protected right to own machine guns, according to a newspaper article that cites a high school student who was present at the talk. [Footnote: DeWayne Wickham, *Scalia Is Wrong on Guns,* BALT. SUN, Apr. 30, 1999, at 27A.]

(It's not necessary to say in the footnote that this is an opinion column, because the title makes this clear.)

4. Transcripts

Transcripts of news programs may seem more reliable than quotes in reporters' articles; you're supposedly getting the speaker's literal, unedited words. But be on guard for three problems:

(a) *Transcribers make mistakes.* One NPR transcript, for instance, contains the puzzling assertion that courts will have to decide "whether a state even makes good religion."[25] What the speaker really said (the speaker was me) was "whether a state even may exclude religion." The *New York Times* likewise once had to run the following correction:

> Because of a transcription error, an article yesterday about Senator Alfonse M. D'Amato's remarks about Judge Lance A.

Ito misquoted the Senator at one point in some editions. In his conversation with the radio host Don Imus, he said: "I mean, this is a disgrace. Judge Ito will be well known." He did not say, "Judge Ito with the wet nose."[26]

When a speaker sounds like he's saying something stupid, it might be the transcriber's fault.

(b) In many radio and television shows, only a sentence or two from a long interview makes it into the program. The risk of being *quoted out of context* thus remains.

(c) Even intelligent and articulate people sometimes misspeak. When writing, they can see their errors and correct them. When speaking, they might not have the airtime to correct themselves, or might not even notice the error, since they don't have a chance to proofread. Thus, even an accurate transcript *might not accurately reflect the speaker's considered judgment.*

So if you do want to quote a transcript as evidence of what the speaker believes or wants to communicate, be careful. If possible, e-mail the speaker to make sure that the quotes are accurate, especially if the quote seems surprising or damning.

5. Web Sites

Web material, like printed material, is *no more reliable than its authors.* For instance, Web-based documents published by U.S. government agencies, such as the Census Bureau, are generally as reliable as these organizations' printed reports, and are generally more timely. A Web page containing a university's student conduct policies is likely to accurately state what the university's written policies actually are. A Web page maintained by an activist group is likely to reliably state the group's views—but it may not reliably describe the underlying facts, just as a pamphlet published by the group may provide a biased view of the facts.

A Web page *maintained by an individual should generally not be seen as reliable by itself,* even if the person is an expert. Individual authors of Web pages often check those pages less carefully than they would check published work. If you want to cite assertions made on a person's Web page, you should:

(a) check the sources yourself and then both cite the sources and give credit to the Web page;

(b) if the sources aren't given, ask the author for the sources; and

(c) at least, if you can't check the statement yourself, confirm that the author still stands by the statement, and has not lost confidence in it.

Because Web pages change often, you should *keep printed copies* of all the pages on which you rely. That way, if the document changes, moves, or vanishes, you'll still have the copy in case someone asks for it.

B. Check the Studies on Which You Rely

Once you find the original study on which you ultimately want to rely, *read it with a skeptical eye*. Pretend that you disagree with the political view that the study buttresses: For instance, if the study concludes that immigration is a net minus for the economy, pretend that you support broad immigration, and try to read the study from that perspective. Can you identify some possible problems, perhaps including the ones discussed later in this chapter? Does the study confound terms that seem similar but are actually different (Part V.D.1, p. 106)? Does it confuse correlation with causation (Part V.H, p. 121)?

Then, *search for criticisms of the study*. Use LEXIS or WESTLAW to find the law review articles that cite the study; search likewise for newspaper references; and search whatever indices are available within the relevant field. (Your law school's or university's research librarians can point you in the right direction.) You can often quickly find what an article's critics say about it, and get a sense for whether you agree with the criticisms.

If you find flaws in the study, you might still be able to rely on it. But you should ask yourself how serious the flaws are; and if you think the study is still valuable, you should acknowledge the flaws and explain why you think the study is sound despite them.

Why do all this? Four reasons:

1. *Accuracy for its own sake.* You should want your article to be correct; honesty requires this, and it will make you feel better about your work.

2. *Persuasiveness.* Many people who read the article will know the flaws in the studies, or at least will know enough about the subject that they'll sense that there might be something wrong. If you acknowledge the flaws but explain why the studies are still basically sound, you might persuade these readers—but if you ignore the problems, you'll lose credibility.

3. *Depth.* Showing your awareness of the possible weaknesses in the data will make the article deeper and more thoughtful, and thus more impressive.

4. *Grade.* Your professor, who's giving you the grade, is probably one of those readers who knows the studies' flaws. Confronting the flaws will get you a better grade than you'd get if you ignored them.

C. *Compromise Wisely*

These suggestions—track down the original source, don't rely on newspaper accounts, e-mail people who are quoted to make sure that the quotes are accurate, check the studies that you cite—are time-consuming, and you might not have much time: Your seminar paper or law review article is due at the end of the semester, you have to study for other classes, and you have to actually write the article.

It's best if you follow all the suggestions given above, because they aren't as time-consuming as they may appear, and they help avoid embarrassing and grade-reducing errors. But if you do need to cut corners, here are a few items to consider in deciding when to do so:

1. *Importance.* If an assertion is one of the significant steps in your chain of reasoning, check it particularly well.

2. *Controversy.* If an assertion seems especially controversial or counterintuitive, make extra sure that you have it right. First, such assertions are more likely to be wrong or exaggerated than the conventional wisdom tends to be. Second, your readers (including the person who is grading you) are more likely to pay close attention to these assertions.

3. *Personal accusation.* If you're claiming that some person or small group of people did something bad or foolish, make sure that you have solid proof. This is partly a matter of fairness to the targets, and partly of self-protection—readers are especially likely to scrutinize such accusations closely.

4. *Ease of finding the original source.* If the original source is easy to find—for instance, if it's a case or a statute—there's no good excuse for relying on a summary in an intermediate source.

5. *Bias.* Information in an opinion piece, or in a law review article written by an advocate for a particular position, is more likely to be unreliable or incomplete than information in a more objective

news story or treatise. (On the other hand, lack of obvious bias is no guarantee of accuracy, or even of real objectivity.)

D. Be Careful with the Terms You Use

1. Avoid False Synonyms

The law is full of terms that sound similar, for instance, murder, killing, and homicide, but that are actually different. These sorts of seeming synonyms can trip you up if you aren't careful.

Here's an example, from the article mentioned on p. 96:

> In 1905 [New York] ... outlaw[ed] the possession of firearms in any public place by the foreign born (New York State 1905). [footnote: Pennsylvania's law forbidding foreign born residents from killing any animal was upheld by the U.S. Supreme Court in [*Patsone*] *v. Pennsylvania*, 232 U.S. 138 (1914).]

The author also mentioned this two more times in the same article, and in three other articles and a book.

It turns out, though, that neither the New York State 1905 source (N.Y. Consolidated Laws, § 1897) nor the statute upheld in *Patsone* disarmed the *foreign born*; they restricted gun ownership by *noncitizens*. That's significantly different, both practically—among males over 21, the only category for which I have seen the data properly broken down, there were over twice as many foreign-born people as noncitizens in 1900—and theoretically:[27] Disarming noncitizens might be evidence of a different attitude towards the right to bear arms (the subject that the author was discussing) than would disarming all the foreign born, citizens included.

This further reinforces the need to check the original sources rather than relying on articles that cite those sources. But it's also a reminder to consider carefully the distinctions between different terms. Under U.S. law, nearly all noncitizens are foreign-born; but not all the foreign born are noncitizens. The two terms are not synonymous, and can't be used interchangeably.

2. Include All Necessary Qualifiers

Legal rules often get compressed to short phrases that omit a lot of detail. Sometimes this is necessary, especially when the rule is tangential to your main point. But when the details of a rule are relevant, you should include all the qualifiers needed to make your discussion accurate.

106

For instance, is it correct to say that *Zacchini v. Scripps–Howard Broadcasting Co.* upheld the right of publicity against First Amendment challenge? Well, the Court did uphold a narrow version of that right— the right to stop others from rebroadcasting one's entire performance— but not the much more commonly invoked broader version, the right to stop others from using one's name or likeness for commercial purposes.[28] So saying that *Zacchini* held that the right of publicity is constitutional, as some do,[29] is a mistake: It fails to acknowledge that the Court considered only the narrower version of the right.

Likewise, if you want to use Justice Holmes' aphorism that the First Amendment doesn't protect people's right to shout fire in a crowded theater, do so correctly: Remember that the phrase is "The most stringent protection of free speech would not protect a man in *falsely* shouting fire in a theatre and causing a panic."[30] People quoting the phrase usually drop the "falsely,"[31] which changes the meaning substantially. (False statements of fact are often constitutionally unprotected; true ones, even if harmful, are generally protected.)

You could argue that even accurately shouting "fire" in a crowded theater is so dangerous that it should be prohibited. But if you want to make that argument, make it explicitly, rather than relying on the authority of a statement that says something quite different.[32]

Omitting necessary qualifiers is closely related to using false synonyms: "Foreign-born," for instance, is a false synonym for "non-citizen," because it omits the qualifier "unnaturalized." Likewise, "the right of publicity" is a false synonym for the right mentioned in *Zacchini*; the terms are used interchangeably in casual asides, but they are in fact quite different.

More broadly, these are all special cases of the careless use of language—the use of terms without thinking hard about what exactly they mean.

3. Use Precise Terms Rather Than Vague Ones

"Almost 1,000 children," an article reports, "die each year from unintentional gunshot wounds."

Exactly what does this mean? At first, the phrase might not even seem vague, but it is: Does "children" refer to minors—people who are younger than 18? This might seem plausible, but actually we rarely call 17–year-olds "children." I suspect that the connotation of "child" is mostly limited to younger people. Does it refer to 0–to–14–year-olds, a range that's commonly used in fatality statistics?[33] Does it refer to pre-teenagers?

In fact, it turns out that the article apparently refers to all 0–to–24–year-olds.[34] This is an outright error, since even the vague term "children" clearly can't mean that.

But even if "almost 1,000 children" referred to some more reasonable age range, the phrase is still vaguer than it should be. Instead of using the vague term "child," either use a more precise term (such as "minor") or indicate the age range, for instance "In 2000, 150 children age 0 to 17 died in the U.S. from unintentional gunshot wounds."[35] This is more informative, and thus more helpful to readers. It may help you yourself think through the matter more carefully. And it may make your article more credible, because it shows that you're a careful researcher who insists on precision.

Being more precise can also show you possible problems with your argument, and help you fix those problems. For instance, once you make explicit that you are talking about all people age 17 or younger, you should wonder: Why are you drawing the line at this age? Does this line fit with the general structure of your claim? For instance, if you're using the statistic as an argument for laws that require that guns be kept unloaded, would such a law affect accidents involving 17–year-olds the same way that it would affect accidents involving 7–year-olds? By using specific terms, you'll more clearly see the relationship between the evidence you're using and the argument you're making.

E. Try To Avoid Foreseeable Misunderstandings by Readers

Guns, one article says, "produce a toll of over 35,000 killed every year and hundreds of thousands more raped, robbed, and assaulted in firearms-related violence." Quick: About how many gun murders were there in 1995, the year that the author was likely talking about?

"Well," you might say, being a careful reader, "we don't know, since the 35,000 might include manslaughter, too." You might even realize that it includes accidents, though you may have been distracted from that by the context, which focuses on "violence." All right then, how many gun murders, manslaughters, and accidental killings were there, put together?

The answer, it turns out, is 17,500. Why? Because 18,500 of the over 35,000 were suicides.[36]

Of course, some readers may believe that suicides should be considered on par with homicides or fatal accidents in determining the costs of gun possession—but others might not. The readers should make this decision for themselves, based on nonmisleading information. In the context of a sentence where the most explicit descriptions are of violent crime ("raped, robbed, and assaulted in firearms-related violence"), many readers will infer that the less explicitly defined term "killed" also refers to criminal killings. This is especially so because the typical reader will be reading the sentence quickly, rather than thinking closely about the various possible literal definitions of each word.

So when you write a sentence, think whether some readers are likely to interpret it as making a different factual claim than you are in fact making. In particular, think about *what assumptions readers are likely to make* based on the context, and make sure that they aren't the wrong assumptions.

F. *Understand Your Source*

Carefully read the source on which you're relying, and understand how all its elements relate to each other. For instance, if you're relying on a statutory section, read the whole statute (or, for vast statutes like the Tax Code, at least all the related sections). Pay especially close attention to the sections containing the definitions, and to other generally applicable provisions that might shed light on the provision that you're considering.

Likewise, if you're looking at a statistical table, make sure you understand what the table discusses:

(a) what *time* the table covers (one year? ten?);

(b) what *geographical or jurisdictional areas* it covers (the whole country? some states? only those states that reported their results to the federal agency? only federal prosecutions?);

(c) what *events* the table covers (all homicides? only solved homicides? only murders?);

(d) what *sources* the table relies on, and what inaccuracies there might be in those sources;

(e) how various line items *relate to each other*.

Consider two examples:

1. Assume that an article says,

[T]he annual accidental death toll for handgun-related incidents is slightly under 200 . . . .

relying on National Safety Council's *Injury Facts* (2000) (1996 data), p. 17, which I reproduce in part on this page. (The actual article relied on an intermediate source.) What's wrong with the quote? The answer is at p. 176.

2. The table on the following page from the *Sourcebook of Criminal Justice Statistics* seems to show that 69.4% of all sexual abuse offenses are committed by "Native Americans, Alaska Natives, Asians, and Pacific Islanders," who together make up 5% of the population.[37] What's the explanation? Again, the answer is at p. 176.

ALL DEATHS DUE TO INJURY, UNITED STATES. 1995-1997, Cont.

Type of Accident or Manner of Injury	1997*	1996	1995
Mechanical suffocation, E913	1,145	1,114	1,062
In bed or cradle, E913.0	236	219	207
By plastic bag, E913.1	44	40	37
Due to lack of air (in refrigerator, other enclosed space), E913.2	21	15	14
By falling earth (noncataclysmic cove-in), E913.3	54	57	59
Other and unspecified mechanical suffocation, E913.8, E913.9	790	783	745
Struck by falling object, E916	727	732	656
Struck against or by objects or persons, E917	247	171	198
Caught in or between objects, E918	85	71	90
Machinery, E919	1,055	926	986
Agricultural machines, E919.0	530	496	514
Lifting machines and appliances, E919.2	119	115	141
Earth moving, scraping, and other excavating machines, E919.7	85	73	106
Other, unspecified machinery, E919.1, E919.3-E919.6, E919.8, E919.9	321	242	225
Cutting or piercing instruments or objects, E920	104	97	118
Firearm missile, E922	981	1,134	1,225
Handgun, E922.0	161	187	233
Shotgun (automatic), E922.1	84	93	116
Hunting rifle, E922.2	65	50	64
Other and unspecified firearm missile, E922.3-E922.9	671	804	812
Explosive material, E923	149	130	170
Fireworks, E923.0	8	9	2
Explosive gases, E923.2	57	49	62
Other and unspecified explosive material, E923.1, E923.8, E923.9	84	72	106
Hot substance or object, corrosive material and steam, E924	111	104	97
Electric current, E925	488	482	559
Domestic wiring and appliances, E925.0	53	66	88
Generating plants, distribution stations, transmission lines, E925.1	139	135	158
Industrial wiring, appliances, and electrical machinery, E925.2	27	15	26
Other and unspecified electric current, E925.8, E925.9	269	266	287
Radiation, E926	0	0	0
Other and unspecified, E914, E915, E921, E927, E928	3,007	2,984	2,730
Late effects (deaths more than one year after accident), E929	1,204	1,126	1,091
Adverse effects of drugs in therapeutic use, E930-E949	248	253	206

Table 5.25

Offenders sentenced in U.S. District Courts under the U.S. Sentencing Commission guidelines

By primary offense, sex, race, and ethnicity, fiscal year 1999

	Sex					Race, ethnicity								
	Total	Male		Female		Total	White		Black		Hispanic[a]		Other[b]	
Primary offense	cases	Number	Percent	Number	Percent	cases	Number	Percent	Number	Percent	Number	Percent	Number	Percent
Total	55,388	46,841	84.6%	8,547	15.4%	54,394	16,728	30.8%	14,246	26.2%	21,231	39.0%	2,189	4.0%
Murder	108	95	88.0	13	12.0	103	29	28.2	18	17.5	17	16.5	39	37.9
Manslaughter	57	38	66.7	19	33.3	57	10	17.5	6	10.5	8	14.0	33	57.9
Kidnaping, hostage-taking	81	77	95.1	4	4.9	80	19	23.8	19	23.8	22	27.5	20	25.0
Sexual abuse	230	226	98.3	4	1.7	229	42	18.3	17	7.4	11	4.8	159	69.4
Assault	455	404	88.8	51	11.2	437	120	27.5	96	22.0	72	16.5	149	34.1
Robbery	1,790	1,638	91.5	152	8.5	1,771	732	41.3	852	48.1	138	7.8	49	2.8
Arson	82	79	96.3	3	3.7	82	60	73.2	10	12.2	3	3.7	9	11.0
Drug offenses														
Trafficking	21,993	18,992	86.4	3,001	13.6	21,780	5,311	24.4	6,743	31.0	9,345	42.9	381	1.7
Communication facility	397	320	80.6	77	19.4	395	120	30.4	137	34.7	130	32.9	8	2.0
Simple possession	689	565	82.0	124	18.0	612	275	44.9	171	27.9	146	23.9	20	3.3
Firearms	2,679	2,570	95.9	109	4.1	2,647	1,064	40.2	1,179	44.5	328	12.4	76	2.9
Burglary, breaking and entering	54	52	96.3	2	3.7	54	14	25.9	10	18.5	2	3.7	28	51.9
Auto theft	189	178	94.2	11	5.8	184	87	47.3	56	30.4	37	20.1	4	2.2
Larceny	2,082	1,322	63.5	760	36.5	1,977	981	49.6	705	35.7	170	8.6	121	6.1
Fraud	6,196	4,517	72.9	1,679	27.1	6,077	3,127	51.5	1,876	30.9	752	12.4	322	5.3
Embezzlement	959	386	40.3	573	59.8	939	519	55.3	272	29.0	80	8.5	68	7.2
Forgery, counterfeiting	1,295	1,008	77.8	287	22.2	1,287	526	40.9	533	41.4	167	13.0	61	4.7
Bribery	196	177	90.3	19	9.7	194	91	46.9	49	25.3	33	17.0	21	10.8
Tax	728	596	81.9	132	18.1	712	519	72.9	83	11.7	53	7.4	57	8.0
Money laundering	1,001	766	76.5	235	23.5	991	442	44.6	166	16.8	321	32.4	62	6.3
Racketeering, extortion	977	893	91.4	84	8.6	961	344	35.8	291	30.3	200	20.8	126	13.1
Gambling, lottery	136	124	91.2	12	8.8	136	112	82.4	6	4.4	5	3.7	13	9.6
Civil rights	81	73	90.1	8	9.9	78	52	66.7	16	20.5	10	12.8	0	X
Immigration	9,659	9,053	93.7	606	6.3	9,531	363	3.8	339	3.6	8,652	90.8	177	1.9
Pornography, prostitution	414	405	97.8	9	2.2	410	347	84.6	24	5.9	22	5.4	17	4.1
Prison offenses	299	270	90.3	29	9.7	289	101	34.9	107	37.0	75	26.0	6	2.1
Administration of justice offenses	866	631	72.9	235	27.1	840	350	41.7	182	21.7	271	32.3	37	4.4
Environmental, wildlife	211	195	92.4	16	7.6	205	160	78.0	6	2.9	24	11.7	15	7.3
National defense	20	17	85.0	3	15.0	20	15	75.0	0	X	2	10.0	3	15.0
Antitrust	44	42	95.5	2	4.5	43	37	86.0	2	4.7	1	2.3	3	7.0
Food and drug	78	67	85.9	11	14.1	76	48	63.2	12	15.8	9	11.8	7	9.2
Other	1,342	1,065	79.4	277	20.6	1,197	711	59.4	263	22.0	125	10.4	98	8.2

Note: The sentencing reform provisions of the Comprehensive Crime Control Act, Public Law No. 98-473 (1984), created the United States Sentencing Commission. The Commission's primary function is to develop and monitor sentencing policies and practices for the Federal courts. On Apr. 13, 1987, the Commission submitted initial Sentencing Guidelines and Policy Statements to Congress. The guidelines became effective on Nov. 1, 1987, and apply to all offenses committed on or after that date. These data are derived from the United States Sentencing Commission's fiscal year 1999 Offender Dataset. The Commission collected information on 55,557 cases sentenced under the Sentencing Reform Act (guideline cases) during fiscal year 1999 (Oct. 1, 1998 through Sept. 30, 1999). Given the nature of the data file and reporting requirements, the following types of cases are not included in the data presented here: cases initiated but for which no convictions were obtained; defendants convicted for whom no sentences were yet issued; defendants sentenced but for whom no data were submitted to the Commission; and cases not sentenced under the Sentencing Reform Act (non-guideline cases).

A case or defendant is defined as a single sentencing event for a single defendant (even if multiple indictments or multiple convictions are consolidated for sentencing).

Multiple defendants in a single sentencing event are treated as separate cases. If an individual defendant is sentenced more than once during the fiscal year, each sentencing event is identified as a separate case. (Source, p. A-4.)

Of the 55,557 guideline cases, some were excluded due to missing information. For sex, 169 cases were excluded due to one or both of the following conditions: missing primary offense category, 149; and missing gender information, 46. For race and ethnicity, 1,163 cases were excluded due to one or both of the following conditions: missing primary offense category, 149; and missing race or ethnicity information, 1,124.

Under drug offenses, "communication facility" refers to the use of a device, such as a telephone, in a drug trafficking offense.

[a]Includes both black and white Hispanics.
[b]Includes Native Americans, Alaska Natives, Asians, and Pacific Islanders.

Source: U.S. Sentencing Commission, *1999 Sourcebook of Federal Sentencing Statistics* (Washington, DC: U.S. Sentencing Commission, 2000), pp. 14, 15. Table adapted by SOURCEBOOK staff.

G. Handle Survey Evidence Correctly

1. What Do Surveys Measure?

Survey evidence is often indispensable, and can be fairly reliable. But many surveys are conducted badly, and even well-conducted surveys are often misinterpreted as measuring things that they don't in fact measure. To avoid relying on bad surveys and misrepresenting good ones, we need to ask: What exactly do surveys measure?

Most precisely, surveys measure only what (1) the surveytakers recorded (2) these particular respondents (3) were willing to say (4) in response to the particular questions they were asked—not very useful. But it also turns out that surveys of a small group can reveal to us the

111

likely answers of a larger group, if (and only if) the respondents are a large enough *randomly selected sample* of the broader group; and this can be far more useful, if it's done right. Understanding these limitations should help us identify several ways that one can err in using surveys, and thus help us figure out how to avoid such errors.

2. Errors in Generalizing from the Respondents to a Broader Group

Surveying a randomly selected sample of a group gives us results that are pretty well generalizable to the whole group. And the survey's accuracy is closely related to the absolute number of people who are asked, not to what percentage of the broader group is surveyed.

That's why you can get a good sense of the views of 280 million Americans by asking even as few as 1000 people. With a randomly selected group of 1000 people, and results ranging from 50%–50% to 80%–20%, you generally get a "margin of error" of ±3%, which means that there's a 95% chance that the actual views of the population at large are within ±3% above or below the result you get from the survey: If the survey says that 42% of respondents say they believe something, there's a 95% chance that the actual number of people who would say they believed that is between 39% and 45%.* The margin of error ends up being roughly 100% divided by the square root of the sample size, so at 100 people the margin is ±10%, and at 2500, it's ±2%.

But—and here's the single most important thing you should remember about surveys—this only works if the respondents *are a randomly selected sample of the whole group*. If the respondents are not a randomly selected sample, or very close to it, then it is mathematically *impossible* to draw an inference from their responses to the likely responses of the whole group.

Unfortunately, several common sample selection techniques violate this assumption:

(a) *Biased samples.* One of the great cautionary tales of surveytaking comes from the 1936 presidential election. The election

---

* Actually, the margin of error is $196\% \times \sqrt{r \times (1 - r)/n}$, where r is the fraction of respondents who lean one way, and n is the number of respondents. Thus, if the split is 50–50, the result is $98\%/\sqrt{n}$; if it's 20–80, the result is $78.4\%/\sqrt{n}$ (since $196\% \times \sqrt{.2 \times .8} = .784$); if it's 10–90, the result is $58.8\%/\sqrt{n}$; and so on.

was won in a 61%–37% landslide by Franklin Roosevelt over Alf Landon, but a vast (2-million-person) *Literary Digest* poll conducted in the weeks before the election showed Landon getting 55% of the vote and Roosevelt 41%.

Part of the problem was simple: The *Literary Digest* pollsters found people's addresses primarily from telephone books and automobile registration records—which means they disproportionately polled richer people. The views of these richer voters may have been quite unrepresentative of the views of all voters.[38]

(b) *Convenience samples.* A special case of this problem is the so-called "convenience sample"—a group of people chosen because they're convenient, such as a professor's freshman psychology students, or a group of pedestrians who pass by the street corner on which a surveytaker is standing. These samples are likewise wildly unrepresentative of the population as a whole: The respondents have a different level of education, they have jobs or interests that lead them to be in a particular place, they come disproportionately from a certain geographical area, and so on.

(c) *Self-selected samples.* The media often publish so-called "self-selected" surveys: For instance, *USA Weekend* once ran a reader poll which asked whether readers thought the nation would be safer if all law-abiding adults were entitled to get a license to carry a concealed weapon. It got 34,000 responses, of which 82% said "yes," a stunning majority in favor of gun decontrol.[39]

But this number is meaningless. First, this sample is obviously biased in one way: It measures only the views of *USA Weekend* readers. Beyond this, though, the survey doesn't even tell us what the average *USA Weekend* reader thought, because only a small and likely unrepresentative fraction of those readers responded. Who takes the time, effort, or money to answer one of these surveys? Likely the people who feel most strongly about the survey topic, and not just average newspaper readers. What's more, many activists tend to e-mail their friends about these polls, so groups that are particularly well-organized on the Internet can quickly swamp the poll results.

Note, incidentally, that the large size of the sample was irrelevant. If you get 34,000 self-selected responses, the result tells you *nothing* about the views of the larger group. But, if you select even 1000 people *randomly* from the country at large, you

113

can get results that are accurate within a range of ±3% (if you do other things right).

(d) *Mail-in samples or Internet samples.* Most mail-in polls and virtually all Internet polls involve self-selected samples, since so few people tend to respond to them. This was another problem with the *Literary Digest* poll: Only 25% of the people who were sent surveys responded, and the respondents' views ended up being quite unrepresentative even of all those who got the surveys.[40]

A mail survey might be made valid, if the surveytakers follow up with all the people who didn't respond, and ultimately get a fairly high response rate. But it's virtually impossible to make a Web-based survey be valid.

So which surveys are indeed valid? First, the surveytakers must try to reach a random sample of a broader group. Second, they must get responses from a majority of the people whom they're trying to reach, to avoid self-selection bias; the best surveys usually have response rates of 70% or above.* Third, they must have a large enough number of respondents to yield a fairly small margin of error: As I mentioned, you'd need 1000 respondents for a ±3% margin, and having a mere 100 respondents will yield a ±10% margin, which is rarely accurate enough.

Most useful surveys involve either random-digit dialing of phone numbers or exit polls (though even exit polls have had serious problems). As I mentioned, the phrases "online survey" and "Internet poll" are almost sure signs of invalidity.

Note that it's especially hard to do surveys of relatively small subgroups of the population, such as Jews or Asians. There's no master list of Jews from which one can draw a random sample, so the best way to poll Jews is to choose a random sample of the population at large, ask respondents whether they are Jewish, and record the answers of the Jews separately from those of the non-Jews. But Jews only make up about 2% of the population, so to get a sample of even 400 people (enough for a ±5% margin of error) you'd need to call 20,000 people—an expensive undertaking.

Some sophisticated polling techniques might make the task more manageable, but it still wouldn't be easy; and, in addition, some respon-

---

* Technically, any response rate below 100% may skew the survey's results, since it may be that the nonrespondents have systematically different views from the respondents; but response rates of 70% are thought to be generally good enough, and ones of as low as 50% are often seen as passable.

dents might not want to reveal their religion or ethnicity to a stranger. So most polls that purport to measure the views of small subgroups tend to have very high margins of error for those subgroups, even if they have a lower margin of error for the population as a whole.

3. Errors in Generalizing from the Question Being Asked

a. Surveys that ask a different question

A survey can *at best* measure people's views on the particular question that was asked; to accurately use a survey, you must therefore properly identify that question. Consider, for instance, how several newspaper and magazine articles summarized the First Amendment Center's *State of the First Amendment 2002* report; I quote one in particular:

> The First Amendment goes too far in guaranteeing free speech, say 49 percent of people polled by the First Amendment Center. The percentage of people who think speech protections are too robust is up some 10 points from 2001.

Seems pretty striking, no? But here's the question that the survey asked:

> The First Amendment became part of the U.S. Constitution more than 200 years ago. This is what it says: "Congress shall make no law respecting an establishment of religion or prohibiting the free exercise thereof; or abridging the freedom of speech, or of the press; or the right of the people peaceably to assemble, and to petition the government for a redress of grievances." Based on your own feelings about the First Amendment, please tell me whether you agree or disagree with the following statement: The First Amendment goes too far in the rights it guarantees.

This question thus did *not* measure people's attitudes towards "guaranteeing free speech," but rather people's attitudes towards the First Amendment as a whole, including the Religion Clauses. It's impossible to tell from this question how many of the 49% thought the speech protections went too far, and how many only thought this about one of the other protections.

And there's good reason to think that much less than 49% of respondents really thought that "speech protections are too robust." A later question in the survey asked people "Overall, do you think Americans have too much freedom to speak freely, too little freedom to speak freely, or is the amount of freedom to speak freely about right?"; only 10% said "too much" (67% said "about right," 21% said "too little," and 1% said they didn't know, or refused to answer). Moreover, some of the respondents were questioned in the days after a Ninth Circuit panel interpreted the Establishment Clause as forbidding schools from using the words "under God" in the Pledge of Allegiance, so it's likely that many respondents were more focused on the establishment of religion than on the freedom of speech. But even setting these speculations aside, saying that 49% of respondents believe that "[t]he First Amendment goes too far in guaranteeing free speech" is just a misreading of what the survey actually asked.

b. Surveys that ask ambiguous questions

If a survey asks questions that different people are likely to interpret differently, then it can't really measure anything in particular.

The *State of the First Amendment* survey, for instance, also asked the following:

> The U.S. Constitution protects certain rights, but not everyone considers each right important. I am going to read you some rights guaranteed by the U.S. Constitution. For each, please tell me how important it is that you have that right . . . . [H]ow important is it that you have the right to privacy?

81% of the respondents said this was essential, and 18% more said it was important; only 1% said it was not important.

Unfortunately, this tells us little about people's actual views. The hottest debates about the right to privacy are, of course, about abortion; but obviously many respondents did *not* interpret the right to privacy as covering abortion rights, since far more than 1% of the public believes that the Constitution should not be read as protecting abortion.

Some people must have thought that "the right to privacy" refers to something else—perhaps the right to be free from unreasonable searches and seizures, or the many other things that are sometimes referred to as "the right to privacy" (some of which are *limitations* on the First Amendment rights of the press). And we have no way of knowing how many people used each possible definition. So virtually everyone thinks that *something* called "the right to privacy" is important, but we don't know what they actually mean by that.

"The right to privacy" is a notoriously ill-defined phrase, but the same can happen with other questions. For instance, another question asked people:

> Many college and university professors currently have the academic freedom to take controversial stands in their classrooms and to publish controversial materials in books and journals. Would you favor or

oppose restrictions on the academic freedom of professors to criticize government military policy during times of war?

41% favored such restrictions, and 56% opposed them.

Unfortunately, there are two questions combined into one here: whether professors should be restricted in *what they say in class* and whether they should be restricted in *what they publish outside class*. (The courts certainly recognize them as different questions—the First Amendment right of public university professors to speak outside class is well-established, but there's a hot debate about whether they have similar rights inside class, especially when their speech is only tangentially related to the subject matter of the class.[41]) Some respondents may have understood the question as focusing mainly on in-class speech. Others may have understood it as focusing mainly on books and articles. Others may have thought it focused on both, and took the same view as to both. Others may have thought it focused on both, and had no way of expressing their different views about both.

So it is a mistake to report, as some newspapers did, that "41 percent [of respondents] said university professors should be restricted from criticizing U.S. military policy during wartime." We don't know what fraction of the respondents actually thought professors should be restricted from criticizing U.S. military policy altogether, and what fraction thought only that professors should be restricted from using their classrooms to do so—a distinction that judges find significant, and that many readers might, too.

c.   Get the text of the questionnaire

To avoid these problems, you should *get the text of the questions* used in any survey on which you want to rely. Many survey organizations release their questionnaires on the Web together with the results (though many media outlets don't fully quote this text); others will give you the questions if you ask them nicely. You should in turn include the text of the relevant question in either the body of the article or the footnotes, where you cite the survey.

If a survey organization refuses to release the questions, then you should be skeptical of the survey's accuracy. You probably shouldn't cite such a survey, and if you do, you should at least alert the reader that the organization refused to release the questions, and that the results of the survey are thus especially hard to evaluate.

4. Errors Caused by Ignoring Information from the Same Survey

Surveys, especially sophisticated ones, often ask many questions and yield a great deal of information. If you use such a survey, it's your responsibility to make sure that you consider all this information, and not just the parts that seem to support your case. And if you rely on a secondary source that uses such a survey, it's your responsibility to make sure that the source has used the survey properly.

Let me return to the *State of the First Amendment* survey, and an article that summarizes it as follows:

> Many Americans, spooked by the Sept. 11, 2001, terrorist attacks on their country, seem inclined to clamp down on First Amendment freedoms, especially freedom of the press . . . .
>
> Each year, the First Amendment Center in Nashville, Tenn.—an independent affiliate of The Freedom Forum—conducts a survey of Americans' attitudes toward the First Amendment . . . .
>
> Among the findings:
>
> * About 49 percent said the First Amendment gives us too much freedom, up from 39 percent last year and 22 percent in 2000.
>
> * The least popular First Amendment right is freedom of the press, with 42 percent saying the news media have too much freedom.
>
> * More than 40 percent of those polled said newspapers should not be allowed to freely criticize the U.S. military's strategy and performance.
>
> * About half said the American press has been too aggressive in asking government officials for information about the war on terrorism . . . .
>
> Freedom of the press exists not only for the news media, but for the very public that it strives to serve. In times when our democratic form of government is under attack, we should fight even harder to preserve our freedoms.

A powerful assertion: People are afraid of terrorism, and they're taking this fear out on the press.

The facts, though, don't fully bear out this story. Here is the fraction of people who think "the press in America has too much freedom to do what it wants" (the 2001 survey was conducted before Sept. 11):

1997	Early 1999	Late 1999	2000	2001	2002
38%	53%	42%	51%	46%	42%

The margin of error is ±3%, so some of the fluctuations may be random, but there's no reason to think that the Sept. 2001 attacks caused *more* people to think the press has too much freedom; in fact, from 2000 to 2002, the fraction of people holding this view *declined* by a statistically significant margin. Likewise, here's the result of another question, which seems to reveal no statistically significant change in attitudes about media freedom from the pre-Sept. 2001 survey to the post-Sept. 2001 survey:

> Some people believe that the media has too much freedom to publish whatever it wants. Others believe there is too much government censorship. Which of these beliefs lies closest to your own?

	2001	2002
Too much media freedom	41%	42%
Too much government censorship	36%	32%
Neither (volunteered)	12%	15%
Both (volunteered)	7%	8%
Don't know/refused	4%	4%

On balance, the rest of the survey likewise doesn't seem to show any material change in public attitudes after Sept. 11, 2001—most differences between the 2001 and 2002 numbers are statistically insignificant, and where the difference is significant, the 2002 numbers tend to be similar to numbers from some of the pre–2001 years. It's hard to explain these results as flowing from a fear of terrorism.

But in any event, those who want to make a case for the claim that "Many Americans, spooked by the Sept. 11, 2001, terrorist attacks ... seem inclined to clamp down on ... freedom of the press," need to confront all the data in the survey, and not just cite the few numbers that seem to support the claim.

5.   Respondents Giving Incorrect Answers to Pollsters

Finally, all this assumes that the respondents answered the questions accurately. This assumption may be wrong for various reasons:

(a) If the question asks about past events, some respondents might not have remembered the events well enough.

(b) Some respondents might have concealed their past behavior (for instance, drug use or gun use) because it's illegal or otherwise embarrassing.

(c) Some respondents might have concealed their present views, for instance, views that they think might be seen by the surveytaker as racist or otherwise unpopular.

(d) Some respondents might have been unwilling to admit their views even to themselves.

(e) Some respondents might have misunderstood even well-designed questions.

(f) Some respondents might not have had firmly held views on the subject, but might have said whatever came to their minds just to avoid looking ignorant or apathetic, either to the surveytaker or to themselves.

Unfortunately, it's not easy to deal with these problems, which is why relying on surveys is risky (though sometimes unavoidable). If you think that a particular survey might yield unsound results because of these problems, look at a good textbook on survey evidence for more information on how serious these problems are likely to be.

6. An Exercise

Here's an exercise, based on a graphic on the front page of the July 16, 2002 *USA Today*; the question refers to a Ninth Circuit case that concluded that the use of the words "under God" in the Pledge of Allegiance violates the Establishment Clause.

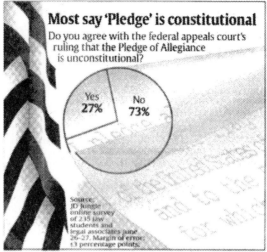

By Lori Joseph and Marcy E. Mullins, USA TODAY

There are at least four errors here (not all of them related just to the statistics); what are they? See p. 176 for the answer.

H. *When Extrapolating, Be Explicit About Your Assumptions*

Policy arguments often implicitly assume that data collected in one situation would apply equally to another situation. For instance, say you're arguing for a proposed federal law, and you cite a study showing that when a similar state law was enacted in Ohio in 1991, robbery arrests fell by 25% in the following year. When you make this argument, you're implicitly making three assumptions:

1. *The data is generalizable over time and space:* You're assuming that results from Ohio in 1991–92 are generalizable to the whole country in the years after the federal law would take effect. Differences among states and changes over time may make this assumption incorrect.

2. *The data shows causation and not just correlation:* You're assuming that arrests fell as a result of the law. That might be true, but it might be a coincidence: arrest rates might have fallen because crime rates were generally falling, or because some other crime-reducing measure was implemented at the same time.

3. *The data is generalizable from the measured variable to the important variable:* You're assuming that a decline in *arrests* reflects a decline in the crime rate, since presumably the goal of the law is to cut crime (the important variable), and not just to cut arrests (the measured variable). A declining arrest rate doesn't necessarily mean a declining crime rate: maybe there was a surge in some other kind of crime, which caused the police to pay less attention to this crime; maybe police practices changed in some other way; maybe the law discouraged people from reporting the crime. This assumption is easy to miss, because the two terms (arrest rate and crime rate) sound similar, though they're actually quite different.

Relying on such assumptions doesn't make your argument fallacious. You might have evidence that shows your assumptions are plausible; and in any event, we often have to make decisions based on hypotheses that are less than mathematically proven.

But you should make your assumptions explicit, and defend them explicitly, so the reader is persuaded that they're justified. You should certainly never hide them by misstatement—or let such common misstatements in others' articles dupe you.

To see these principles more clearly, try the following exercise: Assume that a study showed that 15% of New York drivers aged 16 to 25 drive drunk at least once a month. The Minnesota legislature is considering new penalties for drunk driving by 16–to–18–year–olds, and a commentator who supports the law writes "Drunk driving has reached epidemic proportion among teenagers, with 15% of driving-age teenagers driving drunk at least once a month." What errors or unstated assumptions can you find in this statement? See p. 178 for the answers.

I. Make Sure Your Comparisons Make Sense

People often use comparisons to draw inferences about causation ("women earn 72.3 percent of what men earn in median annual earnings," so we should infer that this roughly measures the amount of sex discrimination by employers) or about costs and benefits ("a gun in the home is 43 times more likely to kill its owner or a friend than an intruder," so we should infer that the costs of gun ownership for the owners exceed its benefits). Such comparisons are often valid steps in your argument, and can be quite effective rhetorically.

But many comparisons that at first sound good collapse on closer examination, either because they don't consider alternative explanations for the disparities, or because they don't sensibly quantify the costs and the benefits.

1. Consider Alternative Explanations for Disparities

Consider one example, a concurrence in the Supreme Court case *Ring v. Arizona*, which argues that juries, not judges, should decide whether to impose the death penalty (an eminently plausible position, which ultimately got seven votes). The opinion summarizes arguments against the death penalty more broadly, and the second-to-last paragraph reads:

> Many communities may have accepted some or all of these claims [that reflect badly on the death penalty], for they do not impose capital sentences. See A Broken System, App. B, Table 11A (more than two-thirds of American counties have never imposed the death penalty since [the death penalty was reaffirmed to be constitutional in 1976] (2,064 out of 3,066), and only 3% of the Nation's counties account for 50% of the Nation's death sentences (92 out of 3,066)). Leaving questions of arbitrariness aside, this diversity argues strongly for procedures that will help assure that, in a particular case, the community indeed believes application of the death penalty is appropriate, not "cruel," "unusual," or otherwise unwarranted.

At the heart of the argument is a comparison—"only 3% of the Nation's counties account for 50% of the Nation's death sentences"—from which the opinion infers that there is a diversity of views about the death penalty.

But one can't simply infer from (1) some counties' imposing more death penalties than other counties to (2) the conclusion that those counties' citizens have different views on the death penalty, because there's an obvious alternative explanation: (3) the counties that impose few death penalties might simply have *few homicides*.

To begin with, many counties have much smaller *populations* than others; there would be few homicides in those counties for that reason alone. Beyond that, many places have lower *per-capita homicide rates* than others, another reason that those places might rarely impose the death penalty.

In fact, in the 3% of American counties that impose the 50% of the death sentences, there were a total of 142,228 homicides in 1973–1995 (according to the table that the opinion itself cites), and according to the Uniform Crime Reports, there were 487,590 total homicides during the same years.[42] Thus, the more accurate way of putting the point was that "The counties that account for 50% of the Nation's death sentences

123

account for 29% [142,228/487,590] of the Nation's homicides"—a much less striking disparity than 50% to 3%.

Curiously, the table that the opinion cites actually lists the county-by-county differences in the death penalty verdicts as a fraction of all homicides. Those differences are indeed huge, ranging, among listed counties with more than 100 homicides, from 3.04/1000 to 128.44/1000, which does suggest that different communities have different views on when the death penalty is proper. (The homicides in the 3.04/1000 county might tend to be less heinous than the ones in the 128.44/1000 county, but that effect isn't likely to be large enough to explain the 40–fold difference in the death penalty imposition rate.)

The opinion's conclusion about the diversity in death penalty views is thus correct. But rather than relying on a comparison that strongly supported its thesis (the county-by-county disparity in death sentences per homicide), the opinion relied on a comparison that didn't support it (the county-by-county disparity in death sentences).

2. Make Sure That Cost/Benefit Comparisons Sensibly Quantify Costs and Benefits

When you present a comparison as part of a cost-benefit analysis, make sure that the two sides of the comparison bear some proportion to the activity's true costs and benefits. Consider the statement that "a gun in the home is 43 times more likely to kill its owner or a friend than an intruder," used to support the assertion that "guns in the home, rather than providing protection and safety, actually increase the risk of injury and death to their owners." This claim is a technically fairly accurate summary of a study (albeit one that was limited to five years in one county) that "noted 43 suicides, criminal homicides, or accidental gun-shot deaths involving a gun kept in the home for every case of homicide for self-protection."[43]

But while the statement is framed as a cost-benefit comparison, it mischaracterizes the benefit. The primary benefit of guns for "protection and safety" isn't killing intruders, but scaring them away; most defensive gun uses don't even involve the gun being shot, and only a tiny fraction involve an intruder being killed.[44]

The comparison between "likely to kill its owner or a friend" and "likely to kill ... an intruder" is thus unhelpful. It is so far removed from measuring the true benefits of gun ownership as well as the true costs—deaths aren't the only possible cost of gun misuse, and suicides (in the study, 37 of the 43 deaths per self-protective homicide) are, to

124

many people, not equivalent to accidental deaths or criminal homicides—that it adds nearly nothing to the discussion. That it originally seems so telling only makes it more misleading.

3. Say How Many Cases the Comparison Is Based on, and How Small Changes in Selection May Change the Result

Imagine someone pointing out that "In the first ninety years of the 20th century, all major American wars began under Democratic presidents." This implicitly compares Democrats and Republicans, and implies that Democratic presidents are more warlike than Republicans.

This assertion (which I have heard in various versions) is potentially misleading in two ways. First, *the claim is based on four data points*: World War I, World War II, the Korean War, and the Vietnam War. It's hard to infer much from four data points, especially since there are so many other factors besides the President's party affiliation that can influence whether a country goes to war. If casual readers aren't explicitly told that the claim is based on just four items, they may miss this important limitation of the comparison.

Second, *if we broadened the sample by a few years* in both directions, we'd get the Spanish–American War (1898) and the Gulf War (1991), both started under Republican Presidents. This doesn't mean that Republicans were somehow more warlike before 1900 and after 1990—but it does show that the seeming pattern may be caused more by the arbitrarily chosen date range than by any genuine difference between the two groups being compared. A conscientious author should tell readers that the result might have been different if only the sample were defined a bit differently, and should explain just why the sample was chosen as it was.

Likewise, say that you're thinking about repeating the following claim (which I've often heard repeated) in your own work:

A BRIEF ASSESSMENT OF THE SUPREME COURT CASES . . .

[A] study of the holdings in religion clause cases reveals far fewer victories for religious outgroups than the dominant story would lead one to expect . . . . As [an earlier article] has trenchantly noted, only Christians ever win free exercise cases. Members of small Christian sects sometimes win and sometimes lose free exercise claims, but non-Christians *never* win . . . .

By comparing Christians, who sometimes win free exercise claims, and non-Christians, who never do, this book excerpt seemingly implies that the Court or the Court's doctrine is somehow more hostile to non-Christians than to Christians.

As literally written, though, the statement "only Christians ever win free exercise cases" is incorrect. *Cruz v. Beto* (1972) upheld a Buddhist prison inmate's right to sue based on a prison's refusing to give him the same opportunity for religious worship as that given to Christian and Jewish inmates. *Church of the Lukumi Babalu Aye v. City of Hialeah* (1993) struck down a city ordinance that discriminated against practitioners of Santeria (an African religion mixed with "significant elements of Roman Catholicism," but one so distant from traditional American Christianity that it can't properly be called a "Christian sect[]"). *Torcaso v. Watkins* (1961) struck down a law that discriminated against atheists on the grounds that it violated the claimant's "freedom of belief and religion" and "religious freedom"; though the case talks both about the Establishment Clause and the Free Exercise Clause, it was largely a free exercise case, and has been cited as such in other leading free exercise cases.

Referring back to the article that the book cites helps explain matters: The article said "the pattern of the Court's results in *mandatory accommodation* cases is troubling because, put bluntly, the pattern is that sometimes Christians win but non-Christians never do" (emphasis added). Mandatory accommodation claims—claims that the government must exempt a religious observer from a generally applicable law—are a subset of free exercise claims. The book mistakenly failed to limit its assertion to accommodation claims.

But even if you paraphrase the book's assertions to focus on mandatory accommodations, there would still be three important points that you should tell your readers.

1. *Tell the reader the size of your set of cases:* It turns out that only five Supreme Court mandatory accommodation claims have been won by the claimants, and these cases have involved only three different kinds of claims: (a) entitlement to unemployment benefits when a person was fired for observing his Sabbath (three of the five cases), (b) entitlement to unemployment benefits when a person was fired for a religiously motivated refusal to work in arms manufacturing, and (c) entitlement to an exemption from a compulsory education law.[45]

   It's hard to infer much from a set this small—but if one wants readers to draw such an inference, one should acknowledge the size of the set, and explain why it's instructive despite its small size.

2. *Tell the reader how the result would have come out had the inquiry been worded a bit differently:* If we ask not who *raised the claims* in the five cases, but rather who *practically benefited* from those cases, we see that the holding of three of the five cases substantially (and perhaps primarily) benefited Jews, not just Christians. In 1963, when the first of these cases was decided, there were apparently under 350,000 American Christians who belonged to the prominent Saturday-observer denominations, but over 500,000 Orthodox Jews—the Jews most likely to observe the Sabbath—and 5 million more non-Orthodox Jews, some of whom may also have observed the Sabbath.[46] The exact numbers of likely claimants are unclear, but many Jews doubtless benefited. And the Justices must have realized this: One of the Justices who heard the first case was Jewish (Justice Goldberg), and just a few years earlier, the Court had dealt with a different kind of claim brought by Jewish Sabbatarians.

So it seems that the focus on the religion of these particular litigants is an arbitrary limitation: If we really want to see whether the Court is biased against non-Christians, we should consider which groups practically benefited from the decisions, and not just who the litigants were. But even if there is some justification for focusing on the particular litigants, this choice should be mentioned and defended (as the cited article, though not the citing book, does), and not just made silently.*

3. *More on telling the reader how the result would have come out had the inquiry been worded a bit differently:* Finally, the focus on the accommodation cases is itself an unexplained limitation of the sample. As we saw, to be literally accurate, your assertion would need to be not "only Christians ever win free exercise cases" but "only Christians ever win mandatory accommodation cases in the Supreme Court"—but the new assertion, while literally accurate, becomes accurate only by excluding *Cruz, Lukumi,* and *Torcaso.*

It's not clear that this exclusion is justified: If the Court were biased against non-Christians, one would expect the bias to show up in the non-accommodation cases as well as in the accommodation ones. But again, even if there's a good reason

---

* Some might argue that Jews are an in-group in modern America, and that decisions benefiting them should be viewed the same way as decisions benefiting Christians. But that was certainly not the view of the book's author, as a discussion on the following page in the book made clear; and in any case, if that's your theory, your discussion should make that explicit.

for treating accommodation cases as unusually probative of the Court's biases, the decision to focus on accommodation cases should be mentioned and defended.

So we can compare the original assertion that you might be tempted to make,

> [O]nly Christians ever win free exercise cases. Members of small Christian sects sometimes win and sometimes lose free exercise claims, but non-Christians *never* win.

to the more accurate, more informative, and less likely to mislead version:

> Only Christian claimants have ever won mandatory accommodation cases before the Supreme Court—five cases total, involving three different religious practices. Some of these cases have also benefited non-Christians who share the same practices (for instance, Jewish Sabbatarians), but the important point is that the particular claimants were Christian, because .... And some non-Christians have won religious freedom cases that didn't involve demands for mandatory accommodation, but the mandatory accommodation cases are the important ones, because ....

The first version is more rhetorically effective, and shorter, than the second. But if you were reading a work to learn about the Court and religious freedom, which of these formulations would you prefer as a reader?

J. A Source–Checking Exercise

The mistakes described above may seem obvious; but it's remarkably easy to make them.

You can learn to avoid these mistakes by trying to spot them in others' articles, for example when you're cite-checking an article for your law journal. Start with the following exercise, drawn entirely from real articles. Do this exercise yourself, and then check your conclusions against the answers on p. 179.

I'll begin with a paragraph from a student article in a Top 5 law review. Critically read it; assume that you are considering relying on it in an article you're writing, and that you are checking the original sources to make sure that you won't embarrass yourself. I first noticed this article when a law professor relied on it in a talk he gave and in an article he wrote.

There are at least seven errors, of varying importance, in this excerpt. Go through the sources—source A and the other sources on which it relies—and try to find these errors.

The student article:

Proponents of manufacturers' liability further argue that handguns are almost useless for self-protection: a handgun is six times more likely to be used to kill a friend or relative than to repel a burglar, and a person who uses a handgun in self-defense is eight times more likely to be killed than one who quietly acquiesces. [Footnote cites source A.]

Source A (which was indeed written by a proponent of manufacturers' liability, so no need to check that), **quoted in relevant part**:

The handgun is of almost no utility in defending one's home against burglars. A Case Western Reserve University study showed that a handgun brought into the home for the purposes of self-protection is six times more likely to kill a relative or acquaintance than to repel a burglar. [Footnote cites source B.] . . . . The handgun is also of questionable utility in protecting against robbery, mugging or assault . . . . The element of surprise the robber has over his victim makes handguns ineffective against robbery . . . . A survey of Chicago robberies in 1975 revealed that, of those victims taking no resistance measures, the probability of death was 7.67 per 1000 robbery incidents, while the death rate among those taking self-protection measures was 64.29 per 1000 robbery incidents. [Footnote cites source C.] The victim was 8 times more likely to be killed when using a self-protective measure than not!

Although handguns possess little or no utility as self-protection devices, some may have a socially acceptable value when properly marketed under restricted guidelines [such as to the police].

Source B (the Case Western study), quoted in relevant part:

During the period surveyed in this study [1958–73 in Cuyahoga County, Ohio], only 23 burglars, robbers or intruders who were not relatives or acquaintances were killed by guns in the hands of persons who were protecting their homes. During this same interval, six times as many fatal firearm accidents occurred in the home.

Source C, the Chicago robbery study, quoted in relevant part:

Of those victims taking no resistance measures, the probability of death was 7.67 per 1000 robbery incidents, while the death rate among those taking self-protection measures was 64.29 per 1000 robbery incidents.

[accompanying table, with some percentages omitted for clarity:]

Method of Victim Self–Protection	Extent of Injury to Victim			
	Death	Injured	None	TOTAL
Physical force	7 (6.1%)	66	41	114
With Weapon Not a gun	0	1	4	5
Handgun	0	2	4	6
Verbal Denial of goods	2 (4.5%)	17	25	44
Verbal Shouting	2 (3.7%)	20	32	54
Flight	7 (18.9%)	10	20	37
Verbal or Phys. Resis. & Flight	0	7	13	20
Unknown	23 (79.3%)	3	3	29
None	7 (0.8%)	132	774	913
TOTAL	48 (3.9%)	258	916	1222

K. Summary

1. Find the original sources, rather than trusting what intermediate sources say about them. Don't rely on what a case, an article, or a reference work says about another case.

2. Be cautious about relying on what lawyers say about history, economics, and other disciplines (or on what nonlawyers say about law). Look at what the authors who work in those disciplines say.

3. Particularly distrust newspapers, and, in large measure, radio and television transcripts.

4. Use words and phrases carefully, making sure you use the precise term instead of false synonyms: Homicide doesn't equal murder, and foreign-born doesn't equal noncitizen.

5. Include the necessary qualifiers: There's a difference between shouting fire and falsely shouting fire.

6. Use precise terms rather than vague ones: "Child" means different things to different people.

7. Carefully check any studies you use.

8. Be explicit about assumptions you make, such as assumptions of:

    (a) *generalizability over time and space* (does a one-year study from one city generalize to the whole country?),

    (b) *causation* (did the study find that A caused B, or only that the two were correlated?), and

(c) *generalizability from the measured variable to the important variable* (do falling arrest rates really mean falling crime rates?).

9. Avoid language that seems likely to mislead some readers.

*

VI. CITE-CHECKING OTHERS' ARTICLES

A. *Recommendations for Cite-Checkers*

Part V applies not just to your own work, but also to articles that you're cite-checking for a law journal.

Cite-checking is important, and should be done thoroughly and thoughtfully. Checking authors' sources is part of what law journals *owe the legal profession*. Lawyers, judges, academics, and students rely on the accuracy of journal articles. (Scholars writing their own articles might check the original sources cited by the articles they read, but most readers don't have the time to do that.) Your journal's name attached to the article is an assurance by the journal that the article has been thoroughly checked.

Checking the sources is part of what you *owe the author*. Most authors count on cite-checkers to help catch their errors before the errors appear in print and become public embarrassments.

Checking the sources is part of what you *owe your fellow journal members* (past, present, and future), because embarrassing errors reflect badly on the journal as well as on the author.

Checking the sources is part of your *legal education*, since it helps you develop a careful and skeptical perspective that will help you in your own legal research and writing. It's easier to find errors in others' work than in your own; checking someone else's work is the best practice you can have for your own article and your future memos or briefs.

Finally, catching an author, especially some respected academic, in an error, and then (politely) suggesting that he correct the error can be *rewarding*—you can justly feel good about preventing embarrassment and misinformation.

So when you're cite-checking, you should look out for the same problems that I outline above:

1. If an article cites an intermediate source, find the original source, check the article's assertion against the original source, and suggest that the author cite the original source as well as the intermediate one.

2. Particularly watch for articles citing newspaper summaries of court decisions, court filings, or empirical studies, or citing law review descriptions of historical, economic, or social science work.

3. Make sure that the article describes facts accurately, without using false synonyms, omitting important qualifiers, or relying on vague terms.

4. To the extent possible, investigate the soundness of the studies on which the article relies. If you see a weakness in the study, or find seemingly cogent criticisms of the study, urge the author to correct or clarify the article, or at least to briefly respond to the objection.

5. Look closely for unstated assumptions that the article makes when it draws inferences from the evidence, and suggest that the author make these assumptions explicit.

6. Think about how readers might misinterpret the article's assertions, and suggest that the author clarify the assertions to avoid such misinterpretations.

Of course, you'll need to use your judgment about how far you should go on all these points—how much effort you should invest in source-checking, how many suggestions you feel comfortable making to the author, and how many of those suggestions you insist on. My recommendations are:

(a) Cite-check thoroughly, since that's part of your duty.

(b) Err on the side of making more suggestions rather than fewer; the author will generally appreciate your input (especially since it represents an objective outside judgment), and, at worst, will just decline some of your proposed changes.

(c) Insist only on those suggestions that you think are needed to prevent genuine errors or very probable reader misunderstandings.

(d) Present your case politely, and leave room for compromise language.

(e) *Never* make corrections without informing the author and giving the author a chance to reject or modify them, even if you think that the corrections are obviously necessary.

Fairly thorough cite-checking is one advantage that law has over other disciplines. In most other fields, editors don't systematically check the article's use of sources, though they might check the overall logic of the argument, and might object to factual claims that they themselves know to be false.

Some of the cautionary examples in Part V came from publications that don't do cite-checking; *Crime and Justice* is a faculty-edited journal that relies on authors to check their own sources, and some of the other sources were books, which generally aren't cite-checked by the publishers. Law review cite-checking isn't perfect (consider the student note that I gave as an example on p. 128), but it's better than nothing. And you can make it better still.

B.   *Recommendations for Law Review Editors*

Few people come to law school as good cite-checkers. Critically checking sources is a skill that incoming law review members need to learn, and law review editorial boards are the ones who must teach it.

The material in Part V and VI.A should be helpful for that. I recommend that you tell all new staffers to read these parts *and to do the exercises in Part V*, on pp. 109, 120, 122, and 128 (and perhaps also the editing exercise in Part IV.M, p. 93). You might tell them to first do the exercises without looking at the answers in Appendix II, and then to compare their results against the answers when they're done. You might also organize a talk in which an editor orally walks the students through those exercises, and explains to them the errors that they were supposed to spot. The site *http://volokh.com/writing* contains some PowerPoint presentations that might be useful for such a talk.

*

VII. PUBLISHING AND PUBLICIZING

You've written your law review article, or you've turned a seminar paper into something publishable. What now? (If you're no longer a student, skip the next two subsections and go straight to Part VII.A.3, p. 139.)

A. *Consider Publishing Outside Your School*

1. You Can

If the journals at your school decide not to publish your work, submit it to other journals at other schools. One student whom I advised circulated two of her articles to the main journals at the top 50 law schools, and to specialty journals at the top 20. On the first, she got three offers from primary journals and three from specialty ones; she accepted an offer from a specialty journal at Harvard. On the second, she got six offers from primary journals and nine from specialty ones, and accepted the one from the *U.C. Davis Law Review*.

Another student got offers for her article from the *Georgetown Immigration Law Journal* and the *Columbia Human Rights Law Review,* both well-respected publications at top-fifteen law schools. (Note, by the way, that "law journal" and "law review" are essentially synonyms.) My brother had an article published in the *University of Pennsylvania Law Review* before he even started law school. Many journals hesitate to publish work by students from other schools, but many will seriously consider it. And many journals are starving for good material.

Remember, you've invested a lot of effort in your article. If you publish it, you'll get a valuable credential, and you might actually help improve the law a little bit. Don't let the opportunity slip away.

2. You Should

What if you do have a chance to publish your article as a student Note at your own school? You might still prefer to send the piece out to be competitively considered by other journals.

This requires some effort, but I think it gives you a better credential, unless your own journal is a primary journal at a Top 20 or so school (e.g., the *Northwestern Law Review*), or perhaps a specialty journal at a Top 5 or so school (e.g., the *Harvard Journal on Legislation*). People who see a home-school Note publication on a resume may assume the student was on the journal, and discount the publication because journals tend to publish their own students' work with less quality screening than they use for outside work. But when people see a publication in a journal at a different school, they'll realize that the article was competitively selected, and might think more highly of it.

Before sending out your article to other journals, you should think about how this will look to your fellow journal members. If they see such behavior as disloyal, then ruining your relationship with them might not be worth the extra credential value of an outside publication. And you certainly should not look for an outside placement *after* you've already agreed to publish in your journal, or even after you've submitted it for consideration by your journal (since such submissions to your own journal usually carry an implicit promise that you'll accept an offer of publication).

But journals ought to *welcome* their members' publishing their work elsewhere—and if they don't see it that way, you should be able to persuade them. First, it's no harm to the journal: A journal's reputation turns on the school's reputation and on the quality of the articles from outside authors, not on the quality of its own students' Notes.

Second, it's good for other students on the journal. If a journal has room for, say, 12 student Notes per year, and 20 people want to publish their pieces, then your placing your good article in another journal means one more open slot for the other students. And third, it's good for the school and for student authors when the students' work is published in outside journals rather than inside ones.

In fact, I think journals (other than the primaries at the top 20 schools and specialty journals at the top 5 schools) should adopt a *policy* of advising their students to send their article out for competitive publication. Not all students will follow this advice; some people won't think that the extra credential is worth the trouble. But students should be encouraged to think that outside publication is better for them, for the school, and for their classmates than publishing in their own journal.

It may be too bad that the world is so credential-conscious; if everyone had enough time, they would actually read people's articles rather than just looking at where they were published. Still, the reality is that the place where a piece was published—and whether it was published at an outside journal, through competitive screening—matters, and both student authors and journal editors should recognize it.

3. Here's How

Here's what you do:

1. Write a one-page cover letter that briefly, clearly, and effectively shows that your article is novel, nonobvious, and useful; see Appendix III.A, p. 185, for an example. You're trying to get journal editors to think, "This is a thoughtful, well-written article on an important topic, and if we publish it, many people will read it and cite it. We should be the ones who snag it, rather than letting it go to our rival journals." (Of course, be more subtle and more concrete than that!) This may sound like mere salesmanship rather than Serious, Dignified Scholarship. But much of life requires good salesmanship; if you have a good idea, you should invest some effort into making sure that people see how good it is.

2. Give the article one more editing and proofreading pass, to make sure that it looks as polished as possible. Ask your faculty advisor to suggest more improvements to the article. Sometimes seeing your willingness to actually publish the piece will persuade the professor to give you some tips that he might have otherwise thought were moot.

While you're proofreading, make sure that the footnotes are in Bluebook format. Rightly or wrongly, many journal editors see good Bluebooking as a sign of professionalism; accommodate their prejudices. Not all law journals follow the Bluebook, but the great majority do, so it makes sense to follow the dominant convention. And journals that don't follow the Bluebook probably get 90% of their pieces in Bluebook form anyway, so they won't resent you for being part of that 90%.

3. Print a neat, readable copy of your article. Format it to look like an already published article: use a proportionally spaced font, nicely formatted footnotes, single spacing, running page heads, a nicely aligned right margin, hyphenation, and so on. This makes your work more readable and more professional-looking. (I've put a sample document template on the Web at *http://volokh.com/writing*.) Some journals claim that they want submissions in other formats—for instance, double-spaced—but I've never gotten any complaints about my method, and I suspect that most editors prefer articles formatted the way I describe.

4. Do not say that you're a student in your cover letter or in the article, though of course do not lie or make misleading statements about your status. Many journals will realize you're still a law student, but no need to rub their noses in this fact.

5. Get the list of journal mailing addresses, which is linked to by *http://volokh.com/writing*. Some journals also let you submit by e-mail—a list of their e-mail addresses is also linked to by *http://volokh.com/writing*—but many do not.

If you do submit by e-mail, keep in mind that e-mail addresses change more often than postal addresses. If an e-mail address looks like a personal address, call the journal or visit its Web site to confirm that the address is still current. Also, regardless of whether the address looks official, watch for "unknown address" messages that you might get in response to your e-mails.

6. The best times to send out your article are March and mid- to late August. April and September are a little worse but generally fine, May through early August are so-so, and October through February are particularly bad.

Most journals' editorial boards serve from March to March, and many well-regarded journals fill up for the year by the end of October, which is why you should avoid October through February. Most journals operate more slowly during the summer, or don't operate at all, which is why May through early August aren't very good. And because manuscripts might stay in journals' inboxes for several weeks before they're read, April and September submissions may run into problems similar to those of May and October submissions.

On the other hand, if the article is especially time-sensitive, send it out as soon as possible. Ask your faculty adviser for guidance on this.

7. Find any specialty journals (for instance, the *UCLA Entertainment Law Review* or the *Yale Journal of Law & the Humanities*) that focus on your area, and send your article and cover letter to them. To find out which specialty journals are best for you, check the list mentioned in item 5, and also ask your faculty adviser.

Most specialty journals are student-edited, but some are faculty-edited, and many faculty-edited journals insist that you not submit to anyone else while they're considering your work; call them to check whether they indeed have this policy. You should generally avoid journals that don't allow simultaneous submissions, since they might not get back to you for months, and during those months you won't be able to send the article anywhere else. On the other hand, sometimes you might have the time to wait (for instance, if you finish the article in December, when many student journals aren't accepting submissions); then you should submit to faculty-edited journals, which are often quite prestigious—but politely ask them how quickly they'll give you an answer.

8. Look up the latest *U.S. News & World Report* rankings of law schools; this list is not a great indicator of schools' quality, but it does give a good sense of their reputations, which is what matters to you here. Send your article to the main journals at all the top 50 schools; if you have to save postage and trim your mailing list, send to the bottom 30 of that list, since the top 20 are indeed not easy to get into. This whole process may sound unpleasantly class-conscious, but there's a pecking order out there, and ignoring it is costly.

Then, a couple of weeks later, send your article to, say, schools 51–100, or even more broadly. If you want to save on postage and effort, you might wait until several weeks after the first wave, in the hope that someone from the first wave will give you an offer during those weeks. But don't just wait until all the journals in your first wave reject you—many of the journals won't send you a rejection notice for many months, and some will never send it.

9. Wait for an offer.

10. If you get an offer, ask how long you have to decide whether to accept it. The journals usually give you from twenty-four hours to two weeks, though they'll sometimes give more. You generally don't have to accept the offer on the spot, though if the journal does insist on an immediate answer, you may want to say yes if the journal is good enough that you doubt you'll do much better.

11. Listen closely to the offer to hear whether they're offering you publication as a student Note, as opposed to as a full-fledged article. Such student Note offers are not as good, though they're better than nothing. If they are just offering to publish your piece as a student Note, call other journals to see if you can get an article offer from a comparably ranked or even slightly lower-ranked journal.

12. a. Call all the journals on your list that are ranked substantially higher, and tell them that you have an offer from the first journal and that you'd like an expedited review. This can often get you an offer from a more prestigious place; it's considered ethically permissible, it's expected (though of course not relished) by the journals, and it's done all the time. If the other journals need more time than the original journal gave you, you might be able to persuade the original journal's editors to give you an extension, especially if you give them something in return (for instance, a promise that you'll shop up the article only to a small set of journals).

This process may seem tacky, and many people have argued that this system, where authors submit articles to many places and then shop up offers to higher-ranked journals, unfairly wastes student editors'

141

time. This may be a good argument, and it might be good if people could come up with another system for doing this.

Still, I feel obligated to give you the advice that's best for you as an author, which is what I'm trying to do here. As a journal editor, you might understandably resent the current system—but until it's changed, as an author you ought to know the most effective way of operating within it. Professors know these rules; you're entitled to know them, too.

b. Unless your original offer was merely for publication as a student Note (see point 11 above) or has a short deadline, you should probably call only those schools that are substantially higher-ranked. There's no real difference between school 30 on the list and school 25, so if #30 gives you an offer first, and gives you plenty of time before the offer expires (at least a week or two), you may want to reward the editors' good taste.

On the other hand, there probably is a real difference in reputation between #30 and #15. (For advice on where to draw the line, talk to your faculty adviser.) Moreover, if #30 gives you a short deadline, you might want to call #29 and better (or even #31–35), hoping to get an offer which can give you more time in which higher-ranked journals can consider your piece.

c. Don't feel embarrassed about trying to shop an offer from a #75 journal to a #1. True, it would be more impressive to the #1 if you were calling to shop up an offer from #10—but any offer is a signal that some readers think well of the article, and in any event there's no real harm to you if the #1 people aren't impressed by your call.

13. Do not renege once you've accepted an offer: It's unethical and bad for your reputation, and with the Internet, word can get around quickly. "Bust a deal," Auntie Entity tells us, "face the wheel"—all the contract law you need to know.* Once you've accepted an offer, call, write, or e-mail the other journals to withdraw your piece from them; that's the kind thing to do, because it saves them the substantial effort of considering your article further. There's an incomplete but still helpful list of journal e-mail addresses at *http://volokh.com/writing*; other journals' e-mail addresses should be available from their Web sites; and the phone numbers and postal addresses are also available at *http://volokh.com/writing*.

---

* MAD MAX 3: BEYOND THUNDERDOME. The civil procedure aspects of the Thunderdome judicial system—especially the trial by com-bat, where the mantra is "Two men enter, one man leaves"—are more controversial.

14. If you get no offer, give your article a few more good editing passes; you'll be amazed how many improvements you can make after a month or two away from the piece. Send the revised version to the next twenty or thirty lower-ranked journals.

If you're resubmitting in the next editorial board year (editorial board years usually run March to March), also send the revised version to the same journals to which you sent the earlier version—sometimes a new editorial board will be willing to publish an article that the old board rejected. (It's rare, but all it costs you is postage and copying.) Repeat until you have an offer. There are over 400 law journals in the U.S.; if your article is at all worthwhile, you'll get it published somewhere.

15. All this is the best advice I have as of the time this book is being published; but check *http://volokh.com/writing* for updates—if there are important changes in the articles market, I will post new recommendations there.

Finally, a word about an inevitable part of this process—*rejection*. Even experienced law professors at top schools generally get rejected by over 90% of the journals to which they submit. I've written over 30 law review articles, half of which were published in top 20 journals, but my submissions still get rejected by the great majority of the places to which I send them.

Rejection is part of the process, and the only way to deal with it is to try to ignore it. Remember that all you need is one acceptance. Remember also that rejections happen for many reasons, and might have nothing to do with the merit of your piece—for instance, the articles editors might prefer other topics, or might be prejudiced against work written by students or even by law clerks or practicing lawyers.

The *worst* thing you can do is let your fear of rejection keep you from circulating the article as widely as possible, or recirculating it if it wasn't picked up the first time around. Remember: It's not personal. It's not about you. It happens to your professors all the time. And no one will know.

B. *Working with Law Journal Editors*

So your article is accepted for publication, whether at your school or elsewhere. Now, the journal will cite-check it, and work with you to edit it. Here are some tips for getting the most out of this process.

1. Have the Right Attitude About Edits

Editors are law students just like you are (or like you recently were). They have some advantages over you: (1) They are probably more objective about the subject and about your writing than you are, so they can see flaws that you might miss. (2) They probably know less about the subject than you do, so they can more easily read things from the average reader's perspective, and see where the article doesn't explain enough things that the reader would need to know. (3) Some of them are better writers than you are, perhaps because they have more pre-law-school writing experience, or are just more talented.

They also have some disadvantages compared to you: (1) They know less about the subject than you do, so some of their suggested changes may be incorrect. (2) Some of them are worse writers than you are, so their suggested changes may be inelegant or even ungrammatical. (3) They're proposing changes and additions to an existing article, and this new material may clash stylistically with the existing material. (4) The article is *your* article, not theirs, so you are entitled to make your point in your style, not their point in theirs.

These observations lead to some suggestions:

(a) *Seriously consider* any claims that something you wrote is un- clear, inadequately proven, unpersuasive, wrong, or inelegant. If your first reaction is to say "no, my way is better," that might just be because you've fallen in love with your own words, and don't see the flaws that the more impartial editors see. You might want to adopt a *presumption in favor of accepting pro- posed edits*—if both your view and the editor's seem reasonable, go with the editor's, which is more objective and closer to the likely view of most readers.

(b) *Consider especially seriously* claims that you're mischaracteriz- ing a source or making an unsound argument. If the editor thinks this is so, then some readers might, too. Moreover, journals are entitled to insist that you correct any substantive mistakes—ensuring academic honesty is part of their job.

(c) *If material needs to be inserted, write it yourself, or at least heavily edit the proposed insertions.* While you should take seriously editors' objections, you should be more skeptical about their proposed solutions, especially suggestions for new wording (new text, new parentheticals for footnotes, a new abstract, and the like). These proposed changes are often good, but they can contain errors, and they can be inconsistent with your article's style. Feel free to heavily edit the proposed insertions, and other proposed changes, or just reject them and write your own insertions instead.

(d) *Look carefully at proposed changes both in the text and in the footnotes.* The footnotes, as well as the text, will be published under your name, and any errors will be your fault. Check the editors' work, just like they will check yours.

(e) *Reject proposed changes that you think make matters worse.* This is your right as the author (unless the unchanged text would be incorrect or misleading), and in my experience most journals acknowledge that it's your right. If, after taking seriously the suggestion, you think the current text is fine and the proposed change is worse, reject the change—change it back yourself, or mark it with a "STET" (the editing term for "change back").

(f) *Investigate suspicious-seeming claims of erroneous usage.* If you think that some objection is unfounded (for instance, if the editors are saying that it's wrong to put a preposition at the end of a sentence, and you disagree), look it up. Check a usage dictionary—for example, *Webster's Dictionary of English Usage, The New Fowler's Modern English Usage,* or Bryan Garner's *A Dictionary of Modern Legal Usage*—or do a LEXIS search to see how reputable publications do this. There are many usage myths (such as the myth that you may not end a sentence with a preposition), and editors sometimes believe them. If the sources say that you are correct, and if on reflection you believe your usage is not just correct but also more readable, then STET the change, and, if asked, politely explain to the editors why you believe you're right.

(g) *Be skeptical about claims of "journal policy."* Generally, when you're making a reasonable request, and the journal responds just with "no, that's against journal policy," that very response is often evidence that the journal doesn't have a better reason for its objection. (It may also be evidence, however, that your request is unreasonable, and the editors are understandably tired of arguing with you about it.) Claims that "we need to maintain consistency within the volume" are also weak. Very few people will read several articles within one volume (or even one issue) of the journal and say "this article contains split infinitives and that one doesn't—how inconsistent."

Obviously, you and the editors might eventually reach an impasse, and you might be the one who has to give in. But don't give in too quickly. If you feel strongly about the issue, say so to the editors, explain why your position is sensible, and explain that the article will be primarily seen as your work, not the journal's. Often, the editors will be persuaded.

(h) *But remember that your article should be readable, not just correct.* If your usage is technically correct, but the editors' proposal is indeed more readable, go along with it. Tip (a)—take proposed changes seriously—is still the most important one, though sometimes, after taking the proposal seriously, you might find yourself rejecting it.

2.   Insist on Seeing All Changes

All the above presupposes that you are aware of all the changes that are being made—as you should be. Politely but firmly ask the editors to mark any changes they make, either on any paper edits that they send you, or through computerized redlining if the edited versions are sent to you electronically. Stress that you'd like to see even tiny changes, and even changes in footnotes.

Most editors are good about showing you all the changes; even if they know they will insist on a change, they know that they should alert you to it and give you a chance to make it the way you want it made. They understand that the article will have your name on it, and that you therefore deserve to sign off on every letter in it.

Unfortunately, editors sometimes neglect this important point, especially when they think that time is short and that some error is particularly glaring. I once got a final round of page proofs a few days before the article was supposed to be sent to the printer, and found that someone had added a whole paragraph to the introduction, without warning me. Had I not been rereading the whole piece carefully, I would have missed the change, and would have had my name attached to some text that I never wrote and never checked. And on top of that, the new paragraph was grammatically incorrect, and was written in a style that jarringly differed from mine.

So politely tell the journal that you need to see all the changes, no matter how minor; and if you see any unannounced changes being made, raise a fuss (again, politely) so that this doesn't happen again.

146

3. Always Keep a Copy of Any Marked–Up Draft You Mail

First, imagine how rotten you'd feel if you spent days marking up a draft, and then the only existing copy of the mark-up got lost in the mail. Second, keeping the copy lets you do what the next subsection suggests.

4. Make Sure Your Earlier Changes Were Properly Entered

Whenever you get a new draft, make sure that any changes that were marked on the previous draft were properly entered. Even the best editors make mistakes when they enter changes—and you and the editors are jointly responsible for catching these mistakes.

5. Use the Opportunity To Edit More Yourself

When a law journal publishes an article, it usually sends you two rounds of edits, and then one or two rounds of page proofs.

This is a great opportunity for you to go through some more editing passes yourself. You should have edited the article thoroughly before handing it in to your professor and before sending it out to the journals. But now you've had a few months away from the piece, so it will be easier for you to read it with new eyes; you may have learned more about the subject since then; and you're now incorporating edits from someone else, and these edits might cause new problems. So reread the whole piece thoroughly each time you get it, and mark it up just as you did in your earlier edits—correct substantive errors, clarify vague points, remove redundancy, and improve the wording.

In some very late editing passes, for instance in the last round of page proofs, the journal may reasonably demand that you limit your changes to the strictly necessary. That's fine; but make sure that even then you reread the piece and find all those strictly necessary changes— it's amazing how many errors can persist undiscovered until the last moment, or be added in the editing process. I know this from personal experience, since one of my published articles contains a footnote that refers to the "freedom of speach."

6. Keep the Copyright, but Grant Nonexclusive Rights

Your goal as an author is to have your piece be as widely read as possible. This means that:

(a) You want to be able to put in on your Web site, either one you have now or one you'll have when your law firm decides that it wants to publicize its associates' written work.

(b) You want to be able to make copies in case you run out of reprints.

(c) You want to be able to e-mail the paper to people who prefer to get it electronically.

(d) You want to be able to reuse your words and your article's structure in future articles on the same theme, or future works based on the article. (This book, for instance, is based on an article I wrote earlier.)

(e) You want to be able to let people photocopy the article for a law school class or a Continuing Legal Education event, and to let them reprint it in practitioner journals or excerpt it in textbooks.

(f) You want to be able to make presentations based on your article, and create handouts, overhead transparencies, or PowerPoint displays to go with the presentations.

If you transfer the copyright to the law journal, you may lose these rights. True, in practice, you might still be able to do what you want, since law journals aren't assiduous at enforcing their copyrights. But if you want to be honest, you'll have to ask the law journal's permission to do some of these things; and some people, such as publishers of textbooks that might include an excerpted version of your article, might insist on that. Who needs the hassle, and the possible expense?

The law journal, of course, does need to get some rights from you. But there's no reason that it needs *exclusive* rights: Student-edited journals are generally heavily subsidized by their schools, and get the rest of their money from subscriptions and issue sales, so they don't really rely on charging people for permission to reprint articles. Even if they do want to charge for this permission, you should fight them, because such charges are against authors' and readers' best interests— and because permission fees are such a small matter to most journals, you usually won't need to fight much.

Here's some sample language that should give both you and the journal what you both need:

> The author conveys to the journal perpetual, unlimited, nonexclusive rights to reproduce, distribute, and display the article, and to authorize others to do the same. The author conveys to the journal the exclusive right to be the first to publish the article in a law journal. The

author promises to clearly state in each copy or presentation that the article was originally published in the journal.

This lets the journal (a) print the piece without fear of copyright liability, (b) put the piece on its own Web site, (c) let LEXIS and WESTLAW put the piece online, and (d) respond to requests for permission to copy or reprint the article, if the request is sent to the journal (as such requests often are). It also assures the journal that you won't scoop it by publishing the article elsewhere first. But it leaves you free to distribute the article broadly, and to reuse your words later.

If the journal for some reason insists on getting the copyright, offer the following compromise:

> The author conveys to the journal perpetual, unlimited, exclusive rights to reproduce, distribute, and display the article, and to authorize others to do the same. The author, however, retains the perpetual nonexclusive right to reproduce, distribute, perform, display, and adapt the article, and to authorize others to do the same (so long as the author clearly states in each copy or presentation that the article was originally published in the journal), except that the journal retains the exclusive right to be the first to publish the article in a law journal.

This will have the same effect that I describe above, but will technically let the journal own the copyright, subject to your rights to use the article.

If the journal resists, point out the various ways that you might want to reuse the article—for instance, the ways mentioned at the start of this subsection—and ask the editors why they would want to bar you from such reuses. My guess is that most editors will realize that they don't want to stop you from doing these things, and will agree to let you keep at least unlimited nonexclusive rights.

If, however, the editors refuse to leave you with unlimited nonexclusive rights to do what you like to the piece, at least try to persuade them to give you the specific rights you need, for instance:

> The author conveys to the journal perpetual, unlimited, exclusive rights to reproduce, distribute, and display the article, and to authorize others to do the same. The journal, however, conveys back to the author perpetual, unlimited, nonexclusive rights to do the following (so long as the author clearly states in each copy or presentation that the article was originally published in the journal):
>
> 1. post the article on the Internet and allow others to do the same;
>
> 2. make and distribute photocopies of reprints;
>
> 3. distribute copies of the article by e-mail.

4. create new articles and other works that are based on the original article;

5. allow others to make copies of the article, or of parts of the article, for classroom use, republication in a book, use in Continuing Legal Education programs, or other purposes;

6. make presentations that are based on the article and that reuse the article's expression, and to produce audiovisual materials related to those talks.

In my experience, some journals only ask for nonexclusive rights in the first place; others ask for exclusive rights, but, if you object, send you an alternate contract that gives them nonexclusive rights; and most others let you change their standard contract to one of the forms that I give above. Only two journals ultimately insisted on denying me the unlimited nonexclusive rights that I wanted, and they eventually agreed to leave me most of the specific nonexclusive rights that I asked for.

You might also want to add the following to your author's footnote, to encourage people to copy the article as broadly as possible:

The author hereby licenses all readers to make unlimited photocopies of the article. For permission to make other copies, please e-mail the author at [if possible, give an e-mail address that you expect will work for at least several years].

This will make it easier for people to make photocopies, while still giving you the chance to check any copying that might involve heavier editing and might thus accidentally quote your article out of context.

C. Publicizing the Article Before It's Published

As soon as your article is accepted by a journal, write a brief abstract and electronically submit the article and the abstract to the Social Science Research Network, *http://www.ssrn.com* (just click on the "Abstract & Paper Submission" button). This way, the article will be publicized even before it's published, and academics will be able to immediately read it, cite it, and possibly even give you valuable advice about it.

Don't wait until your article is published, which could be many months away. If you think your draft needs one more editing pass before you're willing to have people read it, do that extra edit, but don't let it delay you too much: The earlier you promote your ideas, the more influence they'll have, and the more they'll help build your reputation.

You might even want to submit the article before it's accepted by a journal—many scholars do, and label the piece a "Working Paper"—but

I generally wouldn't recommend it: The article's acceptance by a journal will serve as a signal that encourages people to read it, even if they don't know the author and even if they know the author is still a student.

D. Publicizing the Published Article

1. Reprints

Once your piece is published, you want people to read it, or at least to know that it exists. Ideas that are actively promoted are more likely to be adopted. People who actively (but tastefully) promote themselves are more likely to get jobs, either immediately or down the road.

Order at least 100 reprints, though more is better. Reprints tend to run about 50 cents to one dollar for each extra copy beyond a minimum number, so splurge. (Don't just make your own photocopies, unless you have to; nicely bound reprints are generally easier to read and store on a shelf for further reference, and look more professional.)

Distribute the reprints, with a brief descriptive cover letter, to:

(a) All professors at your school whose work is connected, even remotely, to your area.

(b) All professors and lawyers who have helped you. (Did you thank them in your author's note?)

(c) All professors and lawyers whom you cite in your footnotes. Mention in your cover letters the precise place that you cite them. We all like to see our names in print, so we're much more likely to look at the article when we know it cites us.

Don't be shy about sending reprints to people whose work you disagree with. If you're worried that the person might be offended, soften the blow with a nice note, saying something like "I found your viewpoint very provocative, and while I ended up disagreeing with it, it was very useful in helping me sharpen my own point of view." (Thanks to Hazel Glenn Beh for suggesting this wording.)

(d) All lawyers you know who work in the field, including those you met while working as a law clerk, summer associate, or intern.

(e) All law teachers who write treatises and casebooks in the field. Their addresses are in the *AALS Directory of Law Teachers*, which you can find in the library.

(f) The offices of any legislators, lobbyists, or ideological groups that are interested in any legislation to which your article is relevant.

(g) Anyone else who might be in a position to help you spread your ideas.

(h) Anyone else whom you want to impress.

It also helps to personalize the cover letter as much as possible. When you're sending something to law professors, try to connect it (if possible) to each professor's scholarship. When you're sending it to lawyers, stress how your piece can be practically useful to each of them. See Appendix III.B–C (pp. 186–189) for some examples.

2.   Distributing the Article Electronically

When the article is ready to be published, you should get the file containing the final version, so that you can e-mail it to people and so that you can put it up on the Web.

If someone e-mails you to ask for a copy of the article—perhaps because they've seen it cited somewhere, or because you've mentioned it in an e-mail discussion—you want to be able to easily and quickly send the file back to them. This has happened to me often.

It's also helpful to place the file on the Web, either in HTML form (which basically looks like a normal text-filled Web page) or in PDF form (which looks like a printed journal page). That way, you can link to the article from your Web page, either one you already have or one that your firm will put up for you when you're in practice; and when you're discussing related issues in an e-mail, you can easily cite to the article just by linking to it. Readers who don't have free WESTLAW or LEXIS access—practicing lawyers, faculty or students in other disciplines, and lay readers—may be unwilling to pay to read your article, but they might be glad to read it for free. Moreover, reading an article on a Web page is often quicker and easier than reading it on WESTLAW or LEXIS. Again, I've found that many people have read my articles this way.

Most law journals these days do all the formatting themselves, so they will have a Word or WordPerfect file that they can easily e-mail you. Some have the printer do the final edits; you may have to pay the printer some money (usually around $50 or so) to get an electronic copy of that final version.

Then, you need to make sure that you have the legal right to distribute the article electronically. Part VII.B.6, p. 147, explains how you can reserve this right (and others) when you're signing the copyright agreement. But if you have given away all your rights, the journal may still be willing to give you back the right to distribute the piece by e-mail and on the Web—just ask them politely.

Finally, you need to convert the file into HTML or PDF format, and put it up on a Web page. I can't describe this in detail here, but here are three tips:

(a) Many law students and young lawyers know how to do this, and it isn't terribly hard. Ask some computer-savvy friends whether they can help you.

(b) If that fails, the law school's or law library's Web experts might be willing to help, especially if you can persuade your faculty advisor to ask them on your behalf.

(c) If you go work at a law firm, the firm's Web experts might be willing to help, since most firms like to publicize their associates' achievements.

E. Planning the Next Article

After you've published your piece, you might never want to write another law review article again. But if you do want to write more, look back over your article to see where it can lead you.

To begin with, while writing the article you've probably several times thought, "that's an interesting related question, but it's too much for me to take on." For instance, if you wrote an article about religious freedom provisions and drug laws, you might have focused only on the government acting as sovereign (banning all drug possession by everyone) and set aside the government acting as employer (firing employees for consuming drugs) or as proprietor (barring drug use on government property, such as public parks). Dealing with the other areas would have made an already tough project unmanageable.

Consider writing a separate article about one of these questions, especially since you've already educated yourself on the basic field (here, religious freedom). Better yet, consider returning to these questions but at a broader level. Don't just write on government-as-employer and religious drug use, which some might see as too connected to your previous work and thus less impressive. Instead, try writing on government-as-employer and religious freedom more generally, perhaps using drug use as a prominent test case.

153

Likewise, as you were developing your approach to one area, you might have seen connections to other areas (see p. 38): For instance, if you were writing on how waiting periods for gun purchases should be evaluated under state constitutional rights to keep and bear arms, you might have also noticed that your general reasoning could be applied to waiting periods for abortions under state constitutional rights to privacy. This may have been too tangential a point to cover thoroughly in your earlier piece, but why not use your thinking as the basis for a new article, perhaps one on waiting periods and constitutional rights more generally?

So build on what you learned while writing your old work; but make sure that you say something new.

VIII. ACADEMIC ETHICS

A. *Avoiding Plagiarism*

1. The Two Harms of Plagiarism

Everyone knows you shouldn't plagiarize—but what exactly does that mean? For instance, are you safe if you just include a footnote to the original source, or if you paraphrase instead of directly quoting?

Scholars condemn plagiarism for two reasons. First, it's a *fraud on the reader*. When you write as a scholar, you are vouching for your claims' originality, as well as their accuracy. You expect your reputation—and your grade—to be built partly on your creativity. If you lead the reader to believe that some words or ideas are yours when they really aren't, you're duping the reader into giving you more credit than you deserve.

Second, it's an *injury to the people whose work you're copying*. Just as you're trying to impress your reader with your creativity, so other authors were trying to impress the public with theirs. If you take their words without acknowledgment, you're denying them the credit they deserve.

Each of these points is an independent reason why you must give adequate credit. For instance, paraphrasing a Supreme Court opinion from 1813 does no great injury to its author. Even borrowing ideas or text from last year's opinions may not much harm the Justices who wrote them; Justices probably care little about getting credit in law review articles. But if you don't give proper credit, you're wronging your readers by fooling them into thinking that your work is original when it really isn't.

This also explains why the rules for legal practice differ from those for scholarly work. "Law," the old saying goes, "is the only discipline where 'That's an original idea!' is a pejorative." There's nothing wrong with a lawyer copying language from an earlier brief written by other lawyers at the same firm—the judge expects accuracy, not originality, and the other lawyers know that their work is the firm's to use as it likes. But the *rules in scholarly writing are more demanding*.

2. Your Obligations

What exactly are these more demanding rules? You should check any specific policies that your law school or university might have, but here are some general guidelines:

    a. *If you use an idea, give credit in the footnotes.* Acknowledge:

        i.   any source (law review article, case, or what have you) that you're quoting or paraphrasing;

        ii. any source from which you got an idea, even if no one can tell that you got the idea from it;

        iii. any source that you know has expressed the idea first, even if you came up with the idea independently (since the academic convention is that people are entitled to credit for being the first to say something).

This is the fair thing to do. It makes your work seem more scholarly, because it shows that you've done your research. And it greatly decreases your chances of being accused of plagiarism.

Don't worry that giving too many people credit will make your work look derivative. First, readers know that even truly original work necessarily rests on some preexisting material. And, second, if proper attribution would show that your work *is* too derivative, the honest and effective solution is to make your work more original, not to try to hide its lack of originality.

    b. *If you use someone else's words, acknowledge this by using quotation marks (and by giving credit in the footnotes).* Besides giving credit in footnotes for the *ideas* you borrow, you must also make sure that the *words* you use are either your own, or marked with quotes to indicate the borrowing.

    c. *Don't use close paraphrases as a way of avoiding direct quotes.* Really close paraphrasing can also constitute plagiarism. For instance, if instead of quoting the preceding paragraph, you write in your paper

> When you copy another person's text, indicate this via the use of quotes (and through providing acknowledgments in the citations). In addition to providing acknowledgments in citations for the concepts you use, you should likewise ensure that the language you use is either written by you, or indicated with quotation marks to identify the copying.

you've plagiarized the paragraph, even though you've only literally copied a few words: You've taken so much of the structure and choice of concepts that you're still passing off someone else's writing as your own. Rewrite the sentence instead of paraphrasing—it's more honest, and the result will likely be simpler and better tailored to your claim than a close paraphrase would be.

So either quote using quotation marks or, if that seems inelegant, rewrite it in your own words. Then, your words will either be original or properly marked as unoriginal by the quotes; and the idea will be properly attributed by the footnote.

d. *Include the proper attribution in the first draft, rather than waiting for the final draft.* First, some schools treat unattributed quotes or excessive paraphrases as plagiarism even in early drafts, not just in final ones.[47] Second, even if the law school rules only cover final drafts, the instructor might view unattributed material in a first draft as an early warning sign of an attempt to plagiarize—and even if you do everything right in the end, you don't want to be graded by someone who suspects your ethics. Third, including the attribution at the outset prevents your forgetting to do it later; and "I was going to properly attribute the material, but I forgot" is rarely a persuasive defense.

e. *What you needn't do.* You don't have to give people credit in the text; thorough citation in the footnotes is enough to discharge your intellectual debts. What's more, repeatedly saying "Professor X says this, but that's wrong because" can distract from your affirmative point (see p. 36). You need to deal with the counterarguments, but you don't have to make the other commentators the protagonists of your article.

The goal of the text is to convey your ideas to the reader, and the text should be focused on that goal. In legal writing, we can acknowledge our sources in footnotes. There's no need to use the text for that.

3. Copying from Yourself

If you're seeking *law school credit* for a project, and you're reusing work that you did before, you need to clear this with your instructor. Most law schools will probably not let you reuse substantial parts of a project for which you've already gotten school credit; but they might let you reuse parts of an outside project, if your instructor agrees. Get permission up front.

Also, if you're going to rely heavily in *one published work* on *another of your published works*, then you should let your readers know, with a footnote such as "Portions of the discussion in this section are adapted from . . . ." Such a footnote is a matter of politeness and self-interest as well as honesty: You don't want readers to notice a familiar passage and assume that you've copied someone else's work, or to become annoyed that they've been led to reread something they've already read before. Alerting them at the outset is better for them and for you.

B. Being Candid

Candor and accuracy are part of your academic obligations, too. It's unethical to characterize sources in a way that you know is wrong or misleading. You would feel betrayed if a supposedly scholarly source deceived you, and you'd condemn the source's author. You should likewise make sure that your work is never open to this sort of criticism.

And candor is practically useful as well as ethically necessary. Explaining and responding to the weaknesses in the evidence tends to make your work more impressive and ultimately more persuasive. Trying to hide the problems or, worse, mischaracterizing the facts (even by omission or misleading description) will on balance make your work less effective and less worthy of respect.

If your professor suspects you—even without solid proof—of knowing misstatements or omissions of important details, your grade will suffer. At best, the professor will give you the benefit of the doubt and conclude that you've been merely sloppy rather than deceitful; and who wants that as a best case scenario? This, after all, is the person who will be grading your work, and whom potential employers may call when they want a candid evaluation of your qualities (whether or not you list the professor as a possible reference).

The same is true of potential employers who read your work because it's listed on your resume. Some of them will only skim your work casually, and not see the problems; but others will know more about the field than you do, especially if you're looking for a job in the field in which you've been writing. They'll be tolerant of occasional errors—but if they see a pattern of errors that is suggestive of dishonesty, the results can be devastating for you. If you're one of several applicants for a job, even a hint of possible misconduct might be enough to get you rejected.

C. Being Fair and Polite to Your Adversaries

As Part I.C.2.b (p. 46) and Parts IV.K.12 and IV.K.13 (p. 91) mentioned, it's better to be polite and impersonal in your criticisms of your adversaries, and to be candid, fair, and thorough in responding to their arguments. It's the ethical thing to do. It makes your article more persuasive. It makes you look better. And it avoids turning your adversaries into your enemies.

D. Being Fair to the Law Review Editors Who Publish Your Article

You'll be working closely with your law review editors, and you may run into them unexpectedly in your future career. Everything will go much more smoothly if both sides treat the other fairly. Some particular points:

1. Never renege once you've accepted an offer (see p. 142).

2. Don't lie about your credentials.

3. When you're shopping up an offer (see p. 141), be clear and honest about who gave you the offer and what the offer's terms are.

4. After you've accepted an offer, call or e-mail the other journals to withdraw your piece (see p. 142).

5. Comply with the law review's publication schedule, and if you need to be a few days late with some step, let the editors know as soon as possible.

E. Preserving Confidentiality

Make sure that nothing you write violates any of your obligations of confidentiality.

1. If you're working from a memo you wrote while working at a law firm or in a judge's chambers (see p. 44), make sure that (a) you get your past employer's permission (since the entire work may be confidential work product), and that (b) your article doesn't include any client confidences.

2. If you interview anyone for the article, make sure that you clearly tell them that their words—or the information they reveal—may end up in print.

3. If you want to quote an e-mail, fax, or letter that was sent to you personally, you must ask the author for permission; such messages are presumptively confidential. You should do the same if you want to quote a message that was e-mailed to an Internet discussion list. There may be a plausible argument that the message was voluntarily made public, but

159

the matter isn't completely clear, so you're better off erring on the side of checking with the author.

F. Treating Sources Fairly, and Complying with Human Subjects Protection Guidelines

1. Make sure that any sources that you quote agree to be quoted (see above).

2. Before you publish the quotes, check with the sources to make sure that you're not misquoting them, that you aren't quoting them out of context, and that they didn't misspeak.

3. Use of surveys and interviews is often covered by university rules related to human subjects protection. These rules apply not just to medical experiments, but also—much to the surprise of many law professors—to a much broader range of research, including research that relies even partly on surveys and interviews.

The rules are quite complex, so you should check with your university's Human Subjects Protection Committee or Institutional Review Board (or a similarly named institution) before starting any research that involves surveys or interviews. Fortunately, these committees tend to be willing to give exemptions for most surveys that gather information that isn't confidential; but you do need to ask for the exemption beforehand. If you run into trouble with the committee, ask your faculty advisor for help.

G. Making Data Available

If you rely on unpublished data, especially on data that you gathered yourself, be prepared to make it available to other researchers who are trying to check or repeat your work. This isn't strictly an ethical requirement; but if you don't share your data, many people will assume that you have something to hide. Telling people "you don't need to check my data, just trust me" is a good way to lead them not to trust you.

The best approach is to put the data—both any tables that you might already have computerized and scanned versions of any important documents you have uncovered—on your Web page,* and mention the Web page in your footnotes. That way, even readers who don't actually check your data will know that you're making it available to be checked, and will trust you a bit more as a result.

* If you don't know how, see p. 153 for a few tips on getting people to help you.

Putting the material on the Web can also save you time and trouble later, especially since it will decrease the chances that you'll lose the data. Even if no one else will ever check the data, the law review cite-checkers probably will, so you'll in any case need to format it in a way that others can read it. You might as well use a medium—the Web—that will let you do it once, and not have to worry about repeating it each time someone asks you for the information.

Whether or not you put your data on the Web, make multiple copies or printouts of your materials, and keep them in a safe place. Don't just rely on your computer, or you might lose everything to a disk drive crash. And don't rely on the journal's filing system, even if you sent in the unpublished material and the journal labeled it in the footnotes as being "on file with the law review." I haven't investigated the matter closely, but I highly doubt that these files are reliable enough.

*

Conclusion

This book has tried to provide a short but comprehensive guide to academic legal writing, from choosing a topic to publishing and publicizing the finished work. I hope it helps you make your article better, and encourages you to write still more.

Writing and publishing can help you become a better writer, and thus a better lawyer. It can help you become a more successful lawyer, by getting you a good grade, a good board position on your law review, a publication credit, and the clerkships, lawyer jobs, or teaching jobs that these credentials can yield. And it can, even if only slightly, influence the law for the better.

*

APPENDIX I: CLUMSY WORDS AND PHRASES*

Here are some common clunkers, and their simpler, more readable replacements. Naturally, there's some subjectivity in any such list—other writers will doubtless disagree with me about some of these items. Moreover, the replacements aren't always perfect synonyms: Sometimes, for instance, you need to use the clunker as part of a legal term of art (e.g., "a cease and desist letter").

Still, I suspect that nine times out of ten the replacements will be better than the original, and that you should at least consider making the change. Of course, some of these changes also require some grammatical adjustment of other parts of the sentence.

The Web site *http://volokh.com/writing* lets you download a macro that will automatically highlight in your file most of the words and phrases listed here.

A. *Needlessly Formal Words*

> "Short words are best, and the old words when short are the best of all."
>
> —attributed to Winston Churchill

Some words are fancy synonyms for simpler words. Your readers will know these complex words—but such words take more time and effort to process than simple ones. Switching to simpler words will make your work more pleasant to read, and will make it less likely that readers will set it aside.

---

* Sources: much e-mail from many people; Joseph Stevens, *Legal Language, Plain and Simple,* Mo. B. Bull., Mar. 1993, at 4. For an even more thorough list, see Bruce Ross-Larson, Edit Yourself: A Manual for Everyone Who Works with Words (1996).

CLUMSY WORDS AND PHRASES

1. Verbs

acquire	get
advert to	mention
afford	give *(when used in this sense)*
ascertain	find out
assist	help
attempt	try
cease	stop
commence	start
demonstrate	show
desire	want
elucidate	explain *or* clarify
endeavor	try
enquire	ask
evince	show
exit	leave
expend	spend *(when referring to money)*
facilitate	help
indicate	show *or* say *or* mean
inquire	ask
locate	find
negative	negate *or* reject
notify	tell
observe	see *or* watch
obtain	get
opine	say *or* write *(usually)*
permit	let *or* allow
possess	have
procure	get
provide	give
purchase	buy
request	ask
retain	keep
state	say *or* write *(often, but not always)*
substantiate	prove *or* support
utilize	use

166

2. Nouns

ambit	reach *or* scope
consequence	result *or* effect
echelon	level
individual	person *(except when counterposed to a group or a corporation)*
individuals	people
objective	goal
personnel	people
portion	part
remainder	rest *(usually)*

3. Adjectives, Adverbs, Conjunctions, and Prepositions

additional	another *or* more
additionally	also *or* another
adjacent to	next to *or* near
approximately	about
contiguous to	next to
exclusively	only
firstly, secondly, *etc.*	first, second, *etc.*
forthwith	immediately
frequently	often
inter alia	among others *or* among other things
notwithstanding	despite
numerous	many
prior to	before
provided that	if *or* but *or* so long as
said	the *or* this *(e.g., in "said contract")*
subsequent	later
subsequent to	after
subsequently	after *or* later *or* then
sufficient	enough
very	*consider omitting*

B. *Circumlocutions*

These are phrases that talk around the subject instead of getting to the point. They often add unneeded prepositional phrases or other grammatical complexities that make the sentence harder to parse and its substance harder to see.

CLUMSY WORDS AND PHRASES

1. Generally

a bad thing .... bad
a good thing .... good
a large number of .... many
a number of .... some *or* several *or* many *or something more precise*
at present .... now
at the place that .... where
at the present time .... now
at this point in time .... now *or* currently *or* at this point
(rarely) or some such
at this time .... now *or* currently *or some such*
concerning the matter of .... about
does not operate to .... does not
during the course of .... during
during the time that .... while
excessive number of .... too many
for the duration of............. during *or* while
for the reason that .... because
had occasion to................. *omit*
I would argue that .... *omit*
in a case in which .... when *or* where
in accordance with .... by *or* under
in an *X* manner .... *X*ly, *e.g.,* "hastily" *instead of* "in a
hasty manner"
in circumstances in which .... when *or* where
in close proximity .... near
in point of fact .... in fact *(or omit altogether)*
in reference to .... about
in regard to.................... about
in the course of .... during
in the event that .... if
is able to .... can
is cognizant of .... knows *or* is aware of
is lacking in .... lacks
is unable to .... cannot
it could be argued that.......... *replace with an explanation for
why the argument is sound (if
that's what you mean)*
it has been determined that ...... *omit*
it is apparent that .... clearly *or omit*
it is arguable that .... *replace with an explanation for
why the argument is sound (if
that's what you mean)*
it is clear that................. clearly *or omit*
it should be noted that.......... *omit*
most of the time .... usually

168

negatively affect . . . . hurt *or* harm *or* decrease *or some such*
on a number of occasions . . . . often *or* sometimes
on the part of . . . . by
piece of legislation . . . . law *or* statute *or* bill
referred to as . . . . called
serves to X . . . . Xs (e.g., change *"this only serves to strengthen the opposition"* to *"this only strengthens the opposition"*)
sufficient number of . . . . enough
the case at bar . . . . this case
the instant case . . . . this case
the manner in which . . . . how
this case is distinguishable . . . . *all cases are distinguishable; you probably mean* "this case is different"
to the effect that . . . . that
under circumstances in which . . . . when *or* where
with regard to . . . . about

2. Verbs Turned into Nouns or Adjectives

accord respect to . . . . respect
during the pendency of X . . . . while X was pending
for the purpose of doing . . . . to do
has a deleterious effect on . . . . hurts *or* harms
has a negative impact on . . . . hurts *or* harms
is aware that . . . . knows
is binding on . . . . binds
is desirous of . . . . wants
is dispositive of . . . . disposes of
made negative reference to . . . . criticized *or* disagreed with
render assistance . . . . help
was aware that . . . . knew
with regard to . . . . about

3. "The Fact That"

The phrase "the fact that" adds an extra conceptual level; you're not just talking about an event or condition ("John sold the land to Mary"), but rather about the fact that the event or condition occurred ("the fact that John sold the land to Mary"). Sometimes this extra complexity is necessary—but rarely. The phrase can usually be omitted entirely (perhaps with some grammatical adjustment of the following clause, e.g., "John's selling the land to Mary"), or replaced with "that."

because of the fact that .... because
despite the fact that .... despite *or* though
due to the fact that .... because
in light of the fact that .... because *or* given that
owing to the fact that .... because *or* since
the fact that .... that

C. *Redundancies*

These are phrases in which one word simply repeats what is already embodied in another; this is sometimes worth doing for emphasis, but only rarely. If you replace the phrases with their simpler equivalents, you'll find that the result is usually clearer, and no less emphatic.

any and all .... all
cease and desist .... stop (*except in* "cease and desist order" *or* "cease and desist letter")
consensus of opinion .... consensus
each and every .... every
null and void .... void
period of time .... time *or* period
point in time .... time *or* point
provision of law .... law
rate of speed .... speed
still remains .... remains
until such time as .... until

APPENDIX II: ANSWERS TO EXERCISES

A. *Editing Exercises, p. 93*

Let's start by rewriting the opening paragraph of the first paper:

> The Child Firearms Safety Act as currently written is a well intentioned piece of legislation which will likely have little effect on the incidence of minors accidentally killed by handguns. However, with some critical modifications the act could play a significant role in lowering the number of minors lost to handgun accidents each year. These modifications should include: compelling either that the gun be kept in a locked container *or* unloaded; the inclusion of long guns in the Act; and making violation of the Act a felony offense.

1. Consider the first sentence:

> The Child Firearms Safety Act as currently written is a well intentioned piece of legislation which will likely have little effect on the incidence of minors accidentally killed by handguns.

What information does it convey to the reader?

(a) The Act is well-intentioned.

(b) It won't protect minors much from accidental handgun deaths.

Comparing this brief summary with the full sentence shows two areas of flab. First, we see *unnecessary words*. The summary says "the Act" instead of "the Act as currently written," with no loss of clarity: The phrase "as currently written" restates the obvious—mentioning some law generally refers to the law as currently written, unless there's some reason to think otherwise. The author probably wanted to distinguish the current version from the proposed change, but this distinction is clear enough even without the "as currently written." Likewise, "piece of legislation" is a long way to say "law."

Second, we see *an unhelpful idea*. The first sentence in our summary—"the Act is well-intentioned"—doesn't convey much valuable information. Whether the law is well-intentioned is probably as clear to the reader as it is to the writer, and it in any event doesn't much matter, given the terms of the assignment ("write a short memo advising the Senator whether she should vote for the law").

The author probably wanted to acknowledge the drafters' good intentions as a polite gesture, before criticizing their handiwork; but such a gesture is unneeded in a memo to one's boss. Cut these phrases, which leaves us with:

171

The Child Firearms Safety Act will likely have little effect on the incidence of minors accidentally killed by handguns.

2. *Do normal people talk* about things "having little effect on the incidence of" other things? Say instead

The Child Firearms Safety Act probably will not significantly protect minors against fatal handgun accidents.

or

The Child Firearms Safety Act probably will not significantly reduce fatal handgun accidents involving minors.

or

The Child Firearms Safety Act will probably do little to protect minors from fatal handgun accidents.

The bureaucratese noun phrase "incidence of" is cut, and the noun phrase "little effect on"—which doesn't explicitly say what kind of effect you're looking for—is replaced with the verb phrases "will not significantly protect [or reduce]" or "will do little to protect." None of these is perfect, but all are clearer, more concrete, and more active than the original.

3. Consider the second sentence together with the revised first one:

The Child Firearms Safety Act will probably do little to protect minors from fatal handgun accidents. However, with some critical modifications the act could play a significant role in lowering the number of minors lost to handgun accidents each year.

Note the *redundancy*: The first sentence talks about "protect[ing] minors against fatal handgun accidents" (or, in the original version, "hav[ing] little effect on the incidence of . . . fatal handgun accidents"). The second talks about "play[ing] a significant role in lowering the number of minors lost to handgun accidents"—pretty much the same thing.

How about merging the two sentences? True, shorter sentences are usually better than long ones, but eliminating redundancy is generally better still. If we merge the two sentences, we get:

The Child Firearms Safety Act will probably do little to protect minors from fatal handgun accidents unless some critical modifications are made.

The result is shorter, and still communicates the same message: The word "unless" concisely indicates that there's a problem (a lack of "significant protect[ion of] minors," which is the same as a high "number of minors lost to handgun accidents") that will remain until something is done ("some critical modifications are made").

172

We can improve the sentence still further by changing the *bureau-cratese* "unless some critical modifications are made" to the clearer and more colloquial "unless it is modified":

> The Child Firearms Safety Act will probably do little to protect minors from fatal handgun accidents unless it is modified.

4. Let's now look at the new first sentence together with the old third sentence:

> The Child Firearms Safety Act will probably do little to protect minors from fatal handgun accidents unless it is modified. These modifications should include: compelling either that the gun be kept in a locked container *or* unloaded; the inclusion of long guns in the Act; and making violation of the Act a felony offense.

One sentence now ends with "unless it is modified" (originally, it called for "some critical modifications"), and the other begins with "These modifications should include." If we merge them and cut *the repetition*, we get:

> The Child Firearms Safety Act will probably do little to protect minors from fatal handgun accidents unless it is modified to compelling either that the gun be kept in a locked container *or* unloaded; the inclusion of long guns in the Act; and making violation of the Act a felony offense.

The new sentence is shorter than the original two put together, and still not unreadably long.

5. We now need to fix the grammar to match the changes in sentence structure ("it is modified to compell*ing*" is wrong), but in the process we see that the *original grammar was itself flawed*: The three proposed modifications—"compelling"/"inclusion of"/"making"—weren't grammatically parallel. (Editing often exposes logical and grammatical errors that had been obscured by the excess words.) Tidying up the grammar and trimming yet further, we get:

> The Child Firearms Safety Act will probably do little to protect minors from fatal handgun accidents unless it is modified to cover long guns, to treat violations as felonies, and to allow guns to be kept in a locked container *or* unloaded.

Before: 88 words, 454 characters.

After: 42 words, 198 characters.

All the information, fewer than half the words.

Now, on to the second paper's opening paragraph:

> The proposed Child Firearms Safety Act (the "bill") is an inconsequential piece of legislation. Aside from the significant political impact of the bill, it carries little weight and makes little difference. Despite

public misconceptions, the few benefits of the bill, notably the probable slight decrease in the number of childhood gun accidents, do not exceed the drawbacks, such as the inaccessibility of guns during a home invasion and loss of civil liberties. Therefore, unless some strong amendments are made to the bill, I recommend that you oppose the bill.

Here's a quick mark-up of all the word- and phrase-level problems:

The proposed Child Firearms Safety Act [(the "bill")] *[obvious]* is an [inconsequential] *[word choice]* [piece of legislation] *[legalese]*. [Aside from the significant political impact of the bill,] *[throat-clearing/obvious]* it [carries little weight] *[word choice]* and [makes little difference] *[redundant]*. [Despite public misconceptions,] *[throat-clearing]* the few benefits of the bill, notably the probable slight decrease in [the number of] *[not really necessary]* childhood gun accidents, do not exceed the drawbacks, such as the inaccessibility of guns during a home invasion and [loss of civil liberties] *[vague/possibly redundant]*. Therefore, unless some [strong] *[word choice]* amendments are made to [the bill], I recommend that you oppose [the bill] *[repeated phrase]*.*

And here's the text with those problems corrected:

The proposed Child Firearms Safety Act would be ineffective. It will do little good. The few benefits of the bill, notably the probable slight decrease in childhood gun accidents, do not exceed the drawbacks, such

---

* For those who want a detailed explanation:

The parenthetical "(the 'bill')" adds nothing new; in a memo that discusses one bill, it's clear what you're referring to when you say "the Act" or "the bill."

"Inconsequential" isn't quite idiomatic; one can have inconsequential arguments, but one rarely hears of an "inconsequential law."

"Piece of legislation" is usually legalese for "law," "bill," or some such.

"Aside from the significant political impact of the bill" doesn't add anything. The Senator can easily tell what the bill's political impact would be; you have no specialized knowledge on this subject beyond what she has.

Arguments can "carry little weight," but laws are generally not described this way.

"Carries little weight" and "makes little difference" seem, in context, to mean the same thing.

"Despite public misconceptions" doesn't add anything. Sometimes it might, for instance if you were asked to research what the public thinks about the law. But in this problem, you probably don't know anything more about public attitudes than the Senator does.

"Loss of civil liberties" is vague: Does this refer to Second Amendment rights? To Fourth Amendment rights? To a general right to self-defense? If it's either of the first two, it should be made clearer. If it's the third, then the sentence is redundant. I inferred that it was indeed the third, because the paper didn't say anything later about the Second or the Fourth Amendments.

"Strong" is the wrong word to describe amendments.

The phrase "the bill" is repeated in the last sentence; the second occurrence should be changed to "it." That's what pronouns are for.

as the inaccessibility of guns during a home invasion. Therefore, unless some amendments are made to the bill, I recommend that you oppose it.

The revised version is already shorter, but the revisions expose something deeper: The four sentences overlap considerably.

1. The first sentence says the law is ineffective (the original first sentence called it "inconsequential").

2. The second sentence says the same thing, originally by saying that the law "carries little weight" and "makes little difference."

3. The third sentence explains why the law is ineffective, and makes the first two sentences superfluous: Explaining that the law's benefits don't exceed the drawbacks also communicates that the law would on balance be ineffective.

4. The fourth sentence says that the Senator should oppose the law as it is now written, which adds little to the first three sentences.

Here's the text with the fat (the first, second, and most of the fourth sentence) trimmed away:

> I recommend that you oppose the proposed Child Firearms Safety Act. Its few benefits, notably the probable slight decrease in childhood gun accidents, do not exceed the drawbacks, such as the inaccessibility of guns during a home invasion.

This is shorter, and says pretty much all that the original says, but it still lacks force—so did the original, but this revision just shows the weakness more clearly.

And this weakness comes from the second sentence primarily focusing on abstractions ("benefits" and "drawbacks") and not the concrete things to which the abstractions refer ("slight decrease in childhood gun accidents" and "the inaccessibility of guns during a home invasion"). What's more, the second concrete phrase ("the inaccessibility of guns ...") is itself a bit abstract: The real problem isn't "inaccessibility" as such, but the interference with self-defense. While abstractions sometimes work as political rhetoric, intelligent readers are usually more swayed by concrete points.

So here's an alternative:

> I recommend that you oppose the proposed Child Firearms Safety Act. The Act will probably only slightly decrease childhood gun accidents, but will likely make it substantially harder for people to defend themselves and their children against criminals.

This isn't the best possible rewrite, but it's better than the preceding version—and it's *much* better than what we began with.

Before: 89 words, 477 characters.

After: 38 words, 214 characters.

All the information, fewer than half the words.

B. *Understand Your Source, p. 109*

1. The quote said "[T]he annual accidental death toll for handgun-related incidents is slightly under 200," and referred to the *Injury Facts* excerpt copied on p. 109. *Injury Facts* lists 187 accidents as involving handguns, 93 as involving shotguns, 50 as involving hunting rifles, and 804 as involving "Other and unspecified firearm missile."*

Thus, for most fatal gun accidents, the type of gun isn't reported, or the report isn't entered into the databases on which *Injury Facts* relies. "Under 200" is just the number of fatal gun accidents *known* to involve handguns. The actual number of fatal handgun accidents doubtless includes many (maybe most) of the 804 fatal gun accidents categorized as "Other and unspecified." *Understand how the various line items relate to each other.*

2. The *Sourcebook of Criminal Justice Statistics Online* table on p. 111 did say that 69.4% of all sexual abuse offenses in its dataset were committed by "Native Americans, Alaska Natives, Asians, and Pacific Islanders." But the table reports only *federal* prosecutions, as the heading "Offenders sentenced in U.S. District Courts" and the fourth line of the Note reveal.

The overwhelming majority of sexual abuse cases are prosecuted in state court; the main federal law covering sexual abuse is the one that applies to Indian reservations. American Indians thus commit a tiny fraction of all sexual abuse nationwide, but they commit a large fraction of the sexual abuse prosecuted by the federal government. *Understand what jurisdiction your data covers.*

C. *USA Today Survey Report, p. 120*

As the problem mentioned, the question in this graphic refers to a Ninth Circuit case that concluded that the use of the words "under God" in the Pledge of Allegiance violates the Establishment Clause.

---

* The careful reader will have noted that one of the categories is a bit oddly described: There are very few truly automatic shotguns. It turns out that the label is a bit inaccurate; the "shotguns (automatic)" category, a CDC source tells me, includes all shotguns.

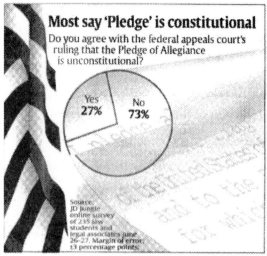

Most say 'Pledge' is constitutional

Do you agree with the federal appeals court's ruling that the Pledge of Allegiance is unconstitutional?

Yes 27% No 73%

Source: JD Jungle online survey of 235 law students and legal associates June 26–27. Margin of error: ±3 percentage points.

By Lori Joseph and Marcy E. Mullins, USA TODAY

1. The first problem isn't with the statistics: The court of appeals didn't rule that "the Pledge ... is unconstitutional"; it ruled that the inclusion of "under God" in the Pledge is unconstitutional. This means that though the current text of the Pledge is impermissible, the Pledge could still be said with two words out of about 30 excised. Simply calling the decision a "ruling that the Pledge of Allegiance is unconstitutional" is likely to mislead quite a few readers.

2. From the text of the headline ("Most say 'Pledge' is constitutional"), most *of whom* did you think said this? When a national paper says "most say," most readers will assume "most Americans," "most citizens," or some such. But the tiny type in the bottom of the box says, "Source: JD Jungle online survey of 235 law students and legal associates June 26–27. Margin of error: ±3 percentage points."

So the survey only measured the views of *law students and legal associates* (whatever "legal associates" exactly means), not a representative sample of the public. Is "Most say 'Pledge' is constitutional" / "Yes 27% / No 73%"—in a paper that isn't aimed at lawyers—an accurate way of summarizing a poll of an uncertain subset of the legal profession?

3. Beyond this, the poll isn't even a valid estimate of the views of "law students and legal associates." The poll is an "online survey," so

it's not a random sample, but a self-selected one: It registers only the votes of those people who hear about the survey and care about it enough to participate—likely those who are unusually interested in the subject, and not a representative sample of *any* group.*

4. Finally, even a random sample of 235 people couldn't yield a margin of error of ±3% (an assurance that there's a 95% chance that the reported result is within 3% of the true breakdown of people's views). If you divide 100 by the square root of 235, you get a margin of error of roughly ±6.5%, and if you're more precise and follow the instructions in the footnote on p. 112, you'll get roughly ±5.8%.

The margin of error only makes sense for randomly chosen samples, not for self-selected ones—but even if we ignore that problem, the ±3% margin of error is incorrect.

D. *Drunk Driving Study, p. 122*

Recall the exercise: Assume that a study showed that 15% of New York drivers aged 16 to 25 drive drunk at least once a month. The Minnesota legislature is considering new penalties for drunk driving by 16–to–18–year-olds, and a commentator who supports the law writes "Drunk driving has reached epidemic proportion among teenagers, with 15% of driving-age teenagers driving drunk at least once a month." What errors or unstated assumptions can you find in this statement?

1. *Generalizing from one place and time to another:* The commentator is making a claim about people generally. Listeners will presumably mean that he's referring either to the nation or to Minnesota, and that he's referring to people now. The commentator should make clear that the numbers refer to New York drivers, at the time the study was conducted. The results might be similar for Minnesotans today, but the reader should be told that this is an assumption, not a proven fact.

2. *Inferring from a group's behavior to the behavior of a subset of the group:* The study focused on behavior among drivers aged 16 to 25, but the commentator is inferring that "driving-age teenagers"—which readers might interpret either as 16–to–18–year-olds, which is what the law refers to, or 16–to–19–year-olds, which is what "driving-age teenagers" literally means (assuming the driving age is 16)—will behave the same way.

This inference may or may not be correct. It may be that 16–to–18–year-olds drink and drive more than 16–to–25–year-olds generally, be-

---

* I called *JD Jungle* and confirmed that the survey was indeed self-selected, as the words "online survey" in the *USA Today* description strongly suggest.

cause they're less mature—or less than 16–to–25–year–olds generally, because they can't legally buy alcohol, or because they're less likely to own a car. In any event, the commentator should again make clear the assumption that he is making.

3. *Misreporting the study:* Finally, the commentator errs in reporting one aspect of the study—the study reported that 15% of New York *drivers* aged 16 to 25 drove drunk at least once a month, not that 15% of 16–to–25–year–olds drove drunk at least once a month. The commentator's ultimate position may be right: There may be a serious drinking and driving problem among Minnesotan teenagers, and perhaps the law will help fight that. But the errors and omissions in reporting the study need to be corrected.

E.   *Source–Checking Exercise, p. 128*

Let's quickly repeat the sources.

The student article:

Proponents of manufacturers' liability further argue that handguns are almost useless for self-protection: a handgun is six times more likely to be used to kill a friend or relative than to repel a burglar, and a person who uses a handgun in self-defense is eight times more likely to be killed than one who quietly acquiesces. [Footnote cites source A.]

Source A (which was indeed written by a proponent of manufacturers' liability, so no need to check that), **quoted in relevant part**:

The handgun is of almost no utility in defending one's home against burglars. A Case Western Reserve University study showed that a handgun brought into the home for the purposes of self-protection is six times more likely to kill a relative or acquaintance than to repel a burglar. [Footnote cites source B.] .... The handgun is also of questionable utility in protecting against robbery, mugging or assault .... The element of surprise the robber has over his victim makes handguns ineffective against robbery .... A survey of Chicago robberies in 1975 revealed that, of those victims taking no resistance measures, the probability of death was 7.67 per 1000 robbery incidents, while the death rate among those taking self-protection measures was 64.29 per 1000 robbery incidents. [Footnote cites source C.] The victim was 8 times more likely to be killed when using a self-protective measure than not!

Although handguns possess little or no utility as self-protection devices, some may have a socially acceptable value when properly marketed under restricted guidelines [such as to the police].

Source B (the Case Western study), quoted in relevant part:

During the period surveyed in this study [1958–73 in Cuyahoga County, Ohio], only 23 burglars, robbers or intruders who were not relatives or acquaintances were killed by guns in the hands of persons who were protecting their homes. During this same interval, six times as many fatal firearm accidents occurred in the home.

Source C, the Chicago robbery study, quoted in relevant part:

Of those victims taking no resistance measures, the probability of death was 7.67 per 1000 robbery incidents, while the death rate among those taking self-protection measures was 64.29 per 1000 robbery incidents.

[accompanying table, with some percentages omitted for clarity:]

Method of Victim Self–Protection	Extent of Injury to Victim			
	Death	Injured	None	TOTAL
Physical force	7 (6.1%)	66	41	114
With Weapon Not a gun	0	1	4	5
Handgun	0	2	4	6
Verbal Denial of goods	2 (4.5%)	17	25	44
Verbal Shouting	2 (3.7%)	20	32	54
Flight	7 (18.9%)	10	20	37
Verbal or Phys. Resis. & Flight	0	7	13	20
Unknown	23 (79.3%)	3	3	29
None	7 (0.8%)	132	774	913
TOTAL	48 (3.9%)	258	916	1222

1. The First Claim

    (i) The first error is small—the clause

    a handgun is six times more likely to be used to kill a friend or relative than to repel a burglar

aims to summarize source A ("a handgun brought into the home for the purposes of self-protection is six times more likely to kill a relative or acquaintance than to repel a burglar"), but replaces "acquaintance" with "friend." The two terms are false synonyms; they sound interchangeable, but they're different—members of rival gangs, for instance, may be acquaintances but not friends, and likewise for a drug dealer and his customer, or a prostitute and her client.* Not that huge a mistake, but worth avoiding all the same.

The more serious problem is that source A errs in quoting source B, which actually says

> During the period surveyed in this study [1958–73 in Cuyahoga County, Ohio], only 23 burglars, robbers or intruders who were not relatives or acquaintances were killed by guns in the hands of persons who were protecting their homes. During this same interval, six times as many fatal firearm accidents occurred in the home.

Let's compare the student article and the original study (source B), noting the differences (tagged in italics):

Student article	Source B
a. "a handgun" *(ii)*	a. "guns"
b. "six times more likely"	b. "six times as many"
c. "to kill a friend or relative" *(iii)*	c. "[to be used in a] fatal firearms accident[]"
d. than "to repel" *(iv)*	d. than to "kill[]"
e. "burglar" *(v)*	e. "burglars, robbers, or intruders who were not relatives or acquaintances"
f. [No place/time specified] *(vi)*	f. Cuyahoga County, Ohio, 1958–73

(ii) The study discusses guns generally, not handguns in particular (item a). Nearly 2/3 of all guns in civilian hands are rifles or shotguns, not handguns.[48] *Make clear when you're inferring from general data* (which covers all guns) *to a specific subset* (handguns).

(iii) The cited study talks about *fatal firearm accidents,* which is not the same as *killings of friends or relatives* (item c). Most uses of firearms to kill a friend or relative are intentional killings, not accidents;[49] and apparently about half of fatal firearm accidents involve the shooter accidentally killing himself, and others involve killings of strangers.[50]

(iv) "Repel[ling] a burglar" is different from "killing" one (item d). One can also repel a burglar with a handgun by visibly pointing it at him, by shooting and missing, or by shooting and wounding—and such

---

* Source A also says "a handgun brought into the home for the purposes of self-protection," rather than just "a handgun," which is how the Harvard article quotes A. But it turns out that the error is in source A, not in the Harvard piece: The original source, B, focused on guns generally, without regard to why they were brought into the home.

uses are probably 50 or more times more common than killings of burglars.[51] *Avoid false synonyms.*

(v) "Burglar" is not the same as "burglars, robbers or intruders who were not relatives or acquaintances" (item e). The difference may not be great, but there is a difference.

(vi) The study is limited to one county and one period (item f). Gun crimes, accidents, and defensive uses vary by place and time; for instance, fatal gun accidents in the U.S. during the study period 1958–73 averaged about 2400/year, while in 1995–99 they averaged a little under 1000/year.[52] It's therefore hard to tell how generalizable the study's findings are, but the article should certainly have acknowledged (at least in a footnote) that the study was limited to gun use in a particular place and time, and not to gun use generally. *Make clear when you're inferring from a specific subset* (Cuyahoga County, 1958–73) *to general data* (the country generally and at all times) *or to another specific subset* (the country in the year that the article was written).

The article said that "Proponents of manufacturers' liability further argue that handguns are almost useless for self-protection . . . ." Can the article's assertions be defended on the grounds that the article is only describing what *proponents are arguing,* not what is in fact true? If so, we shouldn't fault the author of the article being cite-checked, though we'd fault the author of source A.

But I don't think this is right. An author must expect that readers will interpret a statement like this as implicitly endorsing the cited statistics—and the article that we're checking has indeed been cited as endorsing the statistics that it describes. If authors want to cite erroneous sources only to show what others believe, they should explicitly state that the cited material is likely in error: This is part of their *responsibility not to mislead their readers.*

2. The Second Claim

The second claim is that "a person who uses a handgun in self-defense is eight times more likely to be killed than one who quietly acquiesces"; and the article cites source A, which says

> A survey of Chicago robberies in 1975 revealed that, of those victims taking no resistance measures, the probability of death was 7.67 per 1000 robbery incidents, while the death rate among those taking self-protection measures was 64.29 per 1000 robbery incidents. The victim was 8 times more likely to be killed when using a self-protective measure than not!

Here, source A does correctly summarize the original study (source C). But let's compare the student article with source A:

Student article (citing source)	Source A (cited source)
a. [No place/time specified] *(vi½)*	"A survey of Chicago [events] in 1975"
b. [No crime type specified] *(vi½)*	"robberies"
c. "a person who uses a handgun in self-defense" *(vii)*	"[a] victim[] ... taking self-protection measures"
d. "is eight times more likely to be killed"	"[is] 8 times more likely to be killed"
e. "than one who quietly acquiesces"	"[than one who] tak[es] no resistance measures"

(vi½) As in error (vi), source A talks about one place, Chicago, one time, 1975, and one crime, robbery; but the student article talks generally about "a person who uses a handgun in self-defense." The reader should be alerted to this limitation, since the specific data may not apply equally to self-defense more broadly (for instance, to self-defense against burglary, assault, rape, or attempted murder), to the country generally, or to the year that the article was written.

(vii) But the big error is the leap from "self-protection measures" to "us[ing] a handgun in self-defense." Neither source A nor the original study, source C, explicitly equates the relative risk of self-protection measures generally with the relative risk of self-protection using a handgun. *The student article falsely claims something about a specific subset when the data only relates to a broader set.*

Look again at the table from source C:

Method of Victim Self–Protection	Extent of Injury to Victim			
	Death	Injured	None	TOTAL
Physical force	7 (6.1%)	66	41	114
With Weapon Not a gun	0	1	4	5
Handgun	0	2	4	6
Verbal Denial of goods	2 (4.5%)	17	25	44
Verbal Shouting	2 (3.7%)	20	32	54
Flight	7 (18.9%)	10	20	37
Verbal or Phys. Resis. & Flight	0	7	13	20
Unknown	23 (79.3%)	3	3	29
None	7 (0.8%)	132	774	913
TOTAL	48 (3.9%)	258	916	1222

The study found that when a handgun was used for self-protection, *0 out of 6* robberies led to death—not *18 out of 280* (64.29 per 1000), the ratio on which source A relies, and which covers weaponless self-defense, self-defense with weapons, verbal response, and flight. The study doesn't tell us how effective handguns really are for self-defense, since six cases are far too few to justify any inference. But the study also does not show that "a person who uses a handgun in self-defense is eight times more likely to be killed than one who quietly acquiesces."

So the author of the student article made a bad mistake. But the author of source A also erred because his citation of source C is *likely to mislead readers*. Three sentences shortly before the "8 times more likely" sentence and the one sentence immediately after had to do with self-defense using a handgun:

> A Case Western Reserve University study showed that a handgun brought into the home for the purposes of self-protection is six times more likely to kill a relative or acquaintance than to repel a burglar .... The handgun is also of questionable utility in protecting against robbery, mugging or assault .... The element of surprise the robber has over his victim makes handguns ineffective against robbery .... A survey of Chicago robberies in 1975 revealed that, of those victims taking no resistance measures, the probability of death was 7.67 per 1000 robbery incidents, while the death rate among those taking self-protection measures was 64.29 per 1000 robbery incidents. The victim was 8 times more likely to be killed when using a self-protective measure than not!
>
> Although handguns possess little or no utility as self-protection devices, some may have a socially acceptable value when properly marketed under restricted guidelines [such as to the police].

The sentences that cite source C are easily misread as focused on defensive *handgun* uses, rather than on what they literally discuss, which is self-protection generally—and the author of the student article seems to have misread these sentences exactly this way. Had source A explicitly said that it was extrapolating from general self-defense data to handgun data, the student article's author might have recognized the limitations of the data, and at least made them clear to his readers.

Appendix III: Sample Cover Letters

A. *For Sending an Article to Law Reviews*

[Your name]
[Your address]
[Your phone number]
[Your e-mail address]

Articles Department
[Law review name and address]

[Date]

Dear Madam or Sir:

In the attached short article,* I aim to make two contributions. First, I argue that laws requiring bystanders to help crime victims—a hot subject in recent years†—may be practically counterproductive.** The laws' likely practical effects have been largely ignored by the literature, which has focused almost exclusively on whether the laws are morally justifiable.†† As too often happens, discussion about a law's morality has driven out discussion about its wisdom. Such laws have been recently proposed both on the federal level and in some of the largest states; I hope my analysis will help the debate about these

---

* [Note: These footnotes are, of course, explanations for the benefit of this book's readers. You shouldn't include footnotes in your cover letters, or overtly talk about novelty, nonobviousness, or utility—these points should be implicit in your letter, not explicit.]

The piece for which I wrote this letter was unusually short—about 10 pages—and I thought some readers might be troubled by this. I therefore decided to warn readers up front: People's judgments turn in large part on their expectations, so if they are warned to expect something short, they won't mind as much that it's short. Like-

wise, if there's something unusual about your article, you might want to mention it up front.

The article, incidentally, got picked up by a Top 20 primary journal.

† I'm trying to persuade readers that this is a hot field, and that the article will be useful to academics and will thus get cited.

** Saying that a law yields unexpected or counterproductive results tends to highlight that the piece is nonobvious.

†† Suggests that the subject is novel.

185

proposals.***

Second, I hope to start a broader discussion about what I identify as the potential "anticooperative effect" of criminal law and tort law generally: The tendency of some kinds of government coercion, even when they are in the abstract morally proper, to deter citizens from cooperating with the authorities. Sometimes, I suggest, even a morally justifiable urge to legally compel correct behavior can seriously backfire in this way. I hope the example of duty-to-rescue/report laws can stimulate attention to this practical effect of coercive rules.*

Please let me know if you have any questions about the piece.

Sincerely Yours,

[Signature]

B. For Sending a Reprint to Potential Readers

[Your name]
[Your address]
[Your phone number]
[Your e-mail address]

[Recipient name]
[Recipient address]

[Date]

Dear [salutation]:

In the attached short article, I aim to make two contributions, which I hope will be of some use to criminal law teachers.†

*** Aimed at persuading people that this is useful.

* The first paragraph explained the piece's core claim. The second paragraph connects the claim to a broader debate; this is again aimed at persuading readers of the article's academic utility.

† I sent this letter to various criminal law professors, including casebook authors. With the casebook authors, part of my goal was to persuade them to cite the article in the casebook; but I thought it was better to suggest this indirectly.

Though this letter is aimed at professors, the structure would apply equally for any audience, such as lawyers. Quickly say up front that you think the article will be helpful to this particular audience, e.g., tax lawyers; then have a couple of paragraphs

First, I argue that laws requiring bystanders to help crime victims may be practically counterproductive.** The laws' likely practical effects have been largely ignored by the literature, which has focused almost exclusively on whether the laws are morally justifiable. As too often happens, discussion about a law's morality has tended to drive out discussion about its wisdom. I hope my analysis will help broaden both the public, scholarly, and legislative debate about these proposals and class discussions about them.* *[Personalize to the extent possible, e.g., with a sentence such as this:]* Given your work on [subject or article title], which I found to be quite helpful when writing my article and which I cite at p. ____, I thought you might find this topic particularly interesting.

Second, I briefly point to what I call the potential "anticooperative effect" of criminal law and tort law generally: the tendency of some kinds of government coercion, even when they are in the abstract morally proper, to deter citizens from cooperating with the authorities. I freely admit that the magnitude of this effect is hard to gauge, but I argue that the effect must be considered, both as to duty-to-rescue/report laws and as to other laws, such as prostitution laws, illegal immigration laws, and bans on carrying concealed weapons (see pp. ____–____).†

And I hope this discussion may be pedagogically helpful. Students often miss these sorts of indirect practical effects, and discussing the anticooperative effect in this context might help train students to analyze criminal law policy questions more comprehensively.**

I would love to hear any reactions you might have to this piece.

Sincerely Yours,

[Signature]

---

that briefly and clearly explain just how it will be helpful.

** This is a very brief summary of the article's main claim. You might want to summarize your claim in a bit more detail, but remember that this cover letter's purpose is to persuade readers to read the Introduction. If you think one short sentence will do that, stick with the one sentence.

* These sentences are aimed at quickly communicating to the reader that the piece is novel, nonobvious, and useful.

† This connects the main claim to a broader theoretical issue.

** If you think your article has a teaching payoff as well as a scholarship payoff, mention it.

187

C. *For Sending a Reprint to Potential Readers on Whose Work You Substantially Rely*

> [Your name]
> [Your address]
> [Your phone number]
> [Your e-mail address]

[Recipient name]
[Recipient address]

[Date]

Dear [salutation]:

I much enjoyed reading your [article name], and found it very helpful in writing my own article, which I enclose; your article is of course cited heavily on pp. ___-___ [*or "cited heavily throughout," if it is indeed cited throughout the piece*]. [*If you disagree with the recipient's article, write:*] As you may notice, my analysis diverges in some measure from yours, but I nonetheless found your work to be very thought-provoking, and useful in helping me sharpen my own viewpoint.

In my article, I argue that laws requiring bystanders to help crime victims may be practically counterproductive. The laws' likely practical effects have been largely ignored by the literature, which has focused almost exclusively on whether the laws are morally justifiable. As too often happens, discussion about a law's morality has tended to drive out discussion about its wisdom. I hope my analysis will help broaden both the public, scholarly, and legislative debate about these proposals and class discussions about them.

I also briefly point to what I call the potential "anticooperative effect" of criminal law and tort law generally: the tendency of some kinds of government coercion, even when they are in the abstract morally proper, to deter citizens from cooperating with the authorities. I freely admit that the magnitude of this effect is hard to gauge, but I argue that the effect must be considered, both as to duty-to-rescue/report laws and as to other laws, such as prostitution laws, illegal immigration laws, and bans on carrying concealed weapons (see pp. ___-___).

Finally, I hope this discussion may be pedagogically helpful. Students often miss these sorts of indirect practical effects, and discussing the anticooperative effect in this context might help train students to analyze criminal law policy questions more comprehensively.

I would love to hear any reactions you might have to this piece.

Sincerely Yours,

[Signature]

*

ENDNOTES

[1] This discussion builds on Eugene Volokh, *Intermediate Questions of Religious Exemptions—A Research Agenda with Test Suites,* 21 CARDOZO L. REV. 595 (1999); for examples of the incidents on which the test suite is based, *see id.* at 603 n.18 & 630 nn.106–109. *Cf.* KDM *ex rel.* WJM v. Reedsport School Dist., 196 F.3d 1046, 1056–57 (9th Cir. 1999) (Kleinfeld, J., dissenting) (also using computer test suites as a model for testing legal claims).

[2] "We must think things not words, or at least we must constantly translate our words into the facts for which they stand, if we are to keep to the real and the true." Oliver Wendell Holmes, Jr., *Law in Science and Science in Law,* 12 HARV. L. REV. 443, 460 (1899).

[3] *See Insulted Thai Convicted,* L.A. TIMES, Mar. 3, 1988, Metro sec., at 2.

[4] *See* Centers for Disease Control & Prevention, *Injury Mortality Reports, 1999–2000, available at* http://webapp.cdc.gov/sasweb/ncipc/mortrate10.html (query selecting [1] Homicide, [2] Firearm, [3] Year(s) of Report 1999 to 1999).

[5] *See* Pamela Samuelson, *Good Legal Writing: Of Orwell and Window Panes,* 46 U. PITT. L. REV. 149, 165 (1984).

[6] DEIRDRE N. MCCLOSKEY, ECONOMICAL WRITING 33 (2d ed. 2000).

[7] Samuelson, *supra* note 5, at 158.

[8] MCCLOSKEY, *supra* note 6, at 31.

[9] *See* Centers for Disease Control & Prevention, *Injury Mortality Reports, 1999–2000, available at* http://webapp.cdc.gov/sasweb/ncipc/mortrate10.html (query selecting [1] Unintentional, [2] Firearm, [3] Year(s) of Report 2000 to 2000, [unlabeled] custom age range <1 to 14); Centers for Disease Control & Prevention, *WISQARS Nonfatal Injury Reports, available at* http://webapp.cdc.gov/sasweb/ncipc/nfirates2000.html (queries selecting [1] Unintentional, [2] Firearm, [3] Year(s) of Report 2000 to 2000 and Disposition either "Treated and Released" or "Transferred or Hospitalized," [unlabeled] custom age range <1 to 14).

[10] *See* GARRY WILLS, LINCOLN AT GETTYSBURG: THE WORDS THAT REMADE AMERICA 34, 36 (1992).

[11] I owe this example to WEBSTER'S DICTIONARY OF ENGLISH USAGE 640 (1989).

[12] *See id.* I have not checked the source myself (Webster's doesn't give a precise cite), but (1) I trust Webster's, and (2) I couldn't bring myself to omit this example.

[13] The Kentucky 1835 source is listed in the bibliography as "Digest of the Statute Laws of Kentucky. Edited by C.S. Morehead and Mason Brown. 2 vols. Frankfort, Ky.: A.G. Hodges." Because the journal is interdisciplinary, it uses

social science citation conventions rather than those more common in law reviews.

[14] KY. CONST. art. X, § 23 (1799), *in* 3 FRANCIS N. THORPE, THE FEDERAL AND STATE CONSTITUTIONS 1290 (1909).

[15] *Id.* art. III, §§ 28–30, *in* 3 THORPE, *supra* note 14, at 1283–84.

[16] *See id.* art. IX, *in* 3 THORPE, *supra* note 14, at 1288; LEGISLATIVE RESEARCH COMM'N, A CITIZEN'S GUIDE TO THE KENTUCKY CONSTITUTION, *available at* http://www.lrc.state.ky.us/lrcpubs/rr137.pdf, at 159 ("Previous Kentucky Constitutions did not recognize amendments, but required the more elaborate revision process.").

[17] KY. CONST. art. XIII, § 25 (1850) ("That the rights of the citizens to bear arms in defence of themselves and the State shall not be questioned; but the general assembly may pass laws to prevent persons from carrying concealed arms."), *in* 3 THORPE, *supra* note 14, at 1314.

[18] *See* Henry A. Kelly, *Rule of Thumb and the Folklaw of the Husband's Stick,* 44 J. LEGAL EDUC. 341 (1994).

[19] 521 U.S. 844, 877 (1997).

[20] *See* Virginia State Bd. of Pharmacy v. Virginia Citizens Consumer Council, Inc., 425 U.S. 748, 761 (1976).

[21] *See In re* Application of Pacifica Found., 50 F.C.C.2d 1025 (1975) (describing Pacifica as "the licensee of noncommercial educational FM Stations" including "WBAI, New York"); *In re* Citizen's Complaint Against Pacifica Foundation Station WBAI (FM), 56 F.C.C.2d 94 (1975), *eventually aff'd sub nom.* FCC v. Pacifica Found., 438 U.S. 726 (1978) (confirming that the broadcast was indeed on WBAI).

[22] *Marina Wants to Send Too–Salty Sailboat Back to Sea,* VENTURA COUNTY STAR, Apr. 4, 2002, at B01.

[23] *Compare Neighborliness Between Trying Neighbors,* BOSTON GLOBE, Apr. 27, 1997, at E2 ("During a swing through Latin America, another vice president, Dan Quayle, remarked that he wished he had studied Latin so that he could communicate.") *with A Dan Quayle Joke,* WASH. POST, June 1, 1989, at A24 (describing the story's origins).

[24] http://www.c-span.org/search/basic.asp?BasicQueryText=dc + rally + against.

[25] *All Things Considered: Important Supreme Court Decisions From This Past Term,* NAT'L PUB. RADIO, July 3, 2002.

[26] Corrections, N.Y. TIMES, Apr. 7, 1995, at A2.

[27] *See* BUREAU OF THE CENSUS, HISTORICAL STATISTICS OF THE UNITED STATES: COLONIAL TIMES TO 1970 at 116 (1976).

[28] 433 U.S. 562, 573 n.10, 576 (1978) (stressing that the Court was dealing only with the narrow version and not the broad one).

[29] *See, e.g.,* Comedy III Prods., Inc. v. Gary Saderup, Inc., 80 Cal. Rptr. 2d 464, 471 (Ct. App. 1998) (concluding, in a name-or-likeness case, that *Zacchini* "considered, and rejected, a First Amendment defense to liability for infringement of the right of publicity"), *aff'd*, 25 Cal. 4th 387 (2001); Landham v. William Galoob Toys, Inc., 227 F.3d 619, 622 (6th Cir. 2000) ("The right of publicity [speaking of a right to control one's name or likeness] is a creature of state common law and statute and originated as part of the common-law right of privacy. The Supreme Court has recognized its consistency with federal intellectual property laws and the First Amendment, *see generally Zacchini,* ...."). Some law review articles make the same mistake.

[30] Schenck v. United States, 249 U.S. 47, 52 (1919) (emphasis added).

[31] A LEXIS search in the NEWS;US file for "(shouting fire in a theatre or shouting fire in a theater or shouting fire in a crowded theatre or shouting fire in a crowded theater) and date(< 1/1/2002)" yielded 333 results. The same query with "falsely" before the "shouting" yielded only 72. Some of these results were false positives (e.g., stories that used the metaphor more broadly than just in a free speech context, and the occasional story discussing the common omission of "falsely"), but only relatively few.

[32] *Cf.* Editorial, *Misjudgment of "Nuremberg,"* OMAHA WORLD-HERALD, Mar. 30, 2001, at 16 (acknowledging that the Holmes quote was limited to "falsehood," but arguing that it should also apply to speech that implicitly urges the killing of abortion providers).

[33] *See, e.g.,* NATIONAL SAFETY COUNCIL, INJURY FACTS 9 (2000).

[34] The article cites NATIONAL SAFETY COUNCIL, ACCIDENT FACTS (1980), without giving a page number, but the fatal firearms accidents broken down by age range appear on p. 7, where the accidents for children under 5 are given as 60, for age 5 to 14 as 300, and for 15 to 24 as 600. The 1000 figure must thus refer to ages 0 to 24.

[35] *See* Centers for Disease Control & Prevention, *Injury Mortality Reports, 1999–2000, available at* http://webapp.cdc.gov/sasweb/ncipc/mortrate10.html (query selecting [1] Unintentional, [2] Firearm, [3] Year(s) of Report 2000 to 2000, [unlabeled] custom age range <1 to 17).

[36] *See* Centers for Disease Control & Prevention, *Injury Mortality Reports, 1981–1998, available at* http://webapp.cdc.gov/sasweb/ncipc/mortrate9.html (queries selecting [1] All Intents, [2] Firearm, [3] Year(s) of Report 1995 to 1995, and [1] Suicide, [2] Firearm, [3] Year(s) of Report 1995 to 1995).

[37] U.S. Census Bureau, *National Estimates Annual Population Estimates by Sex, Race and Hispanic Origin, available at* http://eire.census.gov/popest/archives/national/nation3/intfile3-1.txt (Nov. 1, 2000 estimates).

[38] *See* Peverill Squire, *Why the 1936 Literary Digest Poll Failed,* 52 PUB. OPIN. Q. 125, 128–30 (1988).

[39] *Vote Now,* USA WEEKEND, Dec. 29–31, 1995, at 5; *Call-in Results,* USA WEEKEND, Feb. 2–4, 1996, at 10.

[40] Squire, *supra* note 38, at 130–31.

[41] *See, e.g.,* Levin v. Harleston, 966 F.2d 85 (2th Cir. 1992) (holding that a professor's writings outside the class are presumptively constitutionally protected); *compare* Dambrot v. Central Mich. Univ., 55 F.3d 1177, 1190 (6th Cir. 1995) ("An instructor's choice of teaching methods does not rise to the level of protected expression.") *and* Cohen v. San Bernardino Valley College, 92 F.3d 968, 971 (9th Cir. 1996) ("Neither the Supreme Court nor this Circuit has determined what scope of First Amendment protection is to be given a public college professor's classroom speech. We decline to define today the precise contours of the protection the First Amendment provides the classroom speech of college professors ....") *with* Hardy v. Jefferson Community College, 260 F.3d 671, 679 (6th Cir. 2001) ("Because the essence of a teacher's role is to prepare students for their place in society as responsible citizens, classroom instruction will often fall within the Supreme Court's broad conception of 'public concern.' ").

[42] U.S. Department of Justice, Bureau of Justice Statistics, *Homicide Trends in the United States, available at* http://www.ojp.usdoj.gov/bjs/homicide/totals.txt.

The comparison in the text isn't quite precise. The table cited by the Supreme Court concurrence counts only "homicides ... occurring during years within the 1973–1995 study period when the state in which the county resides had a valid capital–sentencing statute." When we divide the 142,228 number by the total homicide count throughout the country (487,590), we should presumably adjust the denominator to better match the way the numerator is measured, so the percentage may end up being more than 29%. But 29% is in any event just a rough estimate (for instance, we should probably be dividing not the total homicide counts, but rather the counts of the most serious homicides), and the bottom line would in any event remain the same: The disparity between death sentences and homicides is much less than the concurrence suggests.

[43] Arthur L. Kellermann & Donald T. Reay, *Protection or Peril? An Analysis of Firearms–Related Deaths in the Home,* 314 NEW ENG. J. MED. 1557, 1560 (1986).

[44] *See infra* endnote 51 and accompanying text.

[45] Sherbert v. Verner, 374 U.S. 398 (1963); Hobbie v. Unemployment Appeals Comm'n, 480 U.S. 136 (1987); Frazee v. Illinois Dep't of Emp. Sec., 489 U.S. 829 (1989); Thomas v. Review Bd., 450 U.S. 707 (1981); Wisconsin v. Yoder, 406 U.S. 205 (1972).

[46] WORLD CHRISTIAN HANDBOOK 99–101 (H. Wakelin Coxill & Sir Kenneth Grubb eds., 1962) (estimating the number of Seventh–Day Adventists, Seventh–Day Baptists, and members of the Seventh–Day Church of God); AMERICAN JEWISH COMM., AMERICAN JEWISH YEAR BOOK 63 (1961) (estimating the number of Jews); SAMUEL C. HEILMAN & STEVEN M. COHEN, COSMOPOLITANS & PAROCHIALS: MODERN ORTHODOX JEWS IN AMERICA 2 (1989) ("As a group, [the Orthodox] have for over a generation remained constant at about 10 percent of the American Jewish population of nearly six million."). Of course, some Christian Sabbatari-

ans might not belong to the leading Sabbatarian denominations, and some Christian Sunday observers (such as Frazee in 1989)might take advantage of the religious exemption (though in 1963, many state laws already protected many Sunday observers, even without need for a mandatory Free Exercise Clause accommodation). Nonetheless, there seems to be reason to think that Jews formed the majority of U.S. Sabbath observers in 1963, and very strong reason to think that they at least formed a large fraction of U.S. Sabbath observers.

[47] *See* Terri LeClercq, *Failure to Teach: Due Process and Law School Plagiarism,* 49 J. LEGAL. ED. 236, 254 (1999).

[48] *See* KLECK, TARGETING GUNS, *infra* note 51, at 96–97.

[49] Today, there are over 10 times more total intentional gun killings in the U.S. than fatal gun accidents (though this statistic isn't limited to killings in the home). *See* Centers for Disease Control & Prevention, *Injury Mortality Reports, 1999–2000, available at* http://webapp.cdc.gov/sasweb/ncipc/mortrate10.html (queries selecting [1] Homicide, [2] Firearm, [3] Year(s) of Report 2000 to 2000, yielding 10,801, and selecting [1] Unintentional, [2] Firearm, [3] Year(s) of Report 2000 to 2000, yielding 776). About 20% of the homicides are of family members or boyfriends or girlfriends, and the number seems roughly similar for gun homicides. I have seen no data about the fraction that involves friends (as opposed to acquaintances). *See* U.S. Department of Justice, Bureau of Justice Statistics, *Homicide Trends in the United States—Intimate Homicide, available at* http://www.ojp.usdoj.gov/bjs/homicide/intimates.htm.

Note that the numbers may vary across place and time; for instance, fatal gun accidents have been falling more or less steadily since the mid–1970s, while gun homicides rose sharply in the late 1960s and then fell in the late 1990s. Nonetheless, the disparity is great enough that I suspect intentional gun killings are almost always considerably more common than fatal gun accidents.

[50] According to KLECK, TARGETING GUNS, *infra* note 51, at 294, "about half of unintentional gunshot woundings are self-inflicted"; I've seen no data specifically limited to *fatal* gun accidents, but I see no reason why the results would be markedly different. I know of no data indicating how many fatal accidents involve a shooter accidentally killing a stranger.

[51] A recent study suggests that in over 90% of all defensive gun uses, the assailant isn't even wounded by the defender, much less killed, and another study suggests that only about one in 6.25 gunshot wounds flowing from an assault leads to death. *See* Gary Kleck & Marc Gertz, *Armed Resistance to Crime: The Prevalence and Nature of Self–Defense With a Gun,* 86 J. CRIM. L. & CRIMINOLOGY 150, 185 (1995); GARY KLECK, POINT BLANK: GUNS AND VIOLENCE IN AMERICA 62 (1991). This data is for assaults generally, not for self-defense shootings specifically, but I know of no reason to think that the ratio for self-defense would be significantly higher.

To take another benchmark, guns are *used* in self-defense from 64,000 to 2.5 million times per year, but are used to *kill* in self-defense from 1400 to 3200 times per year. *See* GARY KLECK, TARGETING GUNS 151, 152, 163 (1997) (describing the different estimates). If only half of all defensive uses successfully *repel* an attacker, the ratio between killings and repulsions is still from 10 to 1 (64,000/2/3200) to about 900 to 1 (2.5 million/2/1400). These figures are for all crimes, not just burglaries, but the general point should likely largely hold for burglaries, too.

[52] NATIONAL SAFETY COUNCIL, *supra* note 33, at 42–43; *see* Centers for Disease Control & Prevention, *Injury Mortality Reports, 1999–2000, available at* http://webapp.cdc.gov/sasweb/ncipc/mortrate10.html (query selecting [1] Unintentional, [2] Firearm, [3] Year(s) of Report 1999 to 2000) *and Injury Mortality Reports, 1980–1998, available at* http://webapp.cdc.gov/sasweb/ncipc/mortrate9.html (query selecting [1] Unintentional, [2] Firearm, [3] Year(s) of Report 1996 to 1999).

INDEX

References are to pages.

A

abstractions, 85
acronyms, 91
active voice, 86
addresses of law reviews, 140
administrative agency decisions, 64
"always," 75
"arguably," 79
ATLEAST searches, 66
attorney general opinions, 64

B

background facts and doctrines, 34
balancing, 24
bench memos
    confidentiality, 159
    using in writing article, 44
broadening analysis, 47

C

case notes, 28
checking studies, 104
circuit splits
    and preemption, 30
cite-checking, 133
    studies, 104
    teaching staffers how to cite-check, 135
claim, the, 9
    proving, 35
    stating in introduction, 31
class credit
    checking with professor before reusing work, 45
classmates
    reading your draft, 71
clichés, 87
"compelling state interest," 25
Concepts and Insights series (Foundation), 64
conclusion, 43

concreteness
    importance in proving claim, 35
    in introduction, 31
confidentiality, 159
connecting your claim
    connecting to subsidiary questions, 41
    exporting to broader debates, 40
    exporting to parallel areas, 41
    importing from broader debates, 39
    importing from parallel areas, 40
    when converting practical work into an article, 44
copyright in your article, 147
correlation and causation, 121, 122
cost/benefit comparisons, 124
costs of your proposal
    acknowledging them, 38
counterarguments, 36, 46
    coming up with, 71
cover letters
    to law reviews, 139, 183
    to potential readers, 152, 184, 185
criticizing others, 90, 91

D

deciding what to set aside, 49
deepening analysis, 45
descriptive claims, 9, 10
    avoid just explaining what the law is, 29
distributing article electronically, 152

E

economics sources, 98
editing suggestions
    from classmates, 71
    from law review editors, 144
    from professors, 72
empirical claims, 9, 10, 16
employers
    checking with them before reusing work, 44
enriching your article, 38

197

†